1968

SO-BIJ-165

3 0301 00030558 7

Essays on Milton

Essays on Milton

BY
ELBERT N. S. THOMPSON, Ph.D.

NEW YORK

Russell & Russell

LIBRARY
College of St. Francis
JOLIET, ILL.

FIRST PUBLISHED IN 1914
REISSUED, 1968, BY RUSSELL & RUSSELL
A DIVISION OF ATHENEUM HOUSE, INC.
L.C. CATALOG CARD NO: 68-15179
PRINTED IN THE UNITED STATES OF AMERICA

821.47
T454

Preface

THE essays contained in this volume have been prepared in the belief that some such help is needed either for a first study or a serious reading of Milton's poetry and prose. No one of the essays professes to be a minute study of the subject under discussion. In consequence, footnotes have been given only where they have seemed absolutely essential; and no formal bibliography is included, since the author hopes to publish soon a topical bibliography of Milton. For kind permission to reprint the chapter, "The Theme of *Paradise Lost*," thanks are due the editors of the *Publications of the Modern Language Association of America*. If the essays prove of assistance as an introduction to the work of Milton, their object will be attained.

44228

Contents

Essays on Milton

Essays on Milton

Chapter I

Milton, the "Last of the Elizabethans"

ALTHOUGH the quickening impulse of the Renaissance had scarcely begun, in 1575, to revive the flagging spirit of English poetry, and although civil and religious dissensions deflected from literature talents that otherwise would have been devoted to her service, so that the first real harvest of the new poetry was delayed until the sixteenth century was three quarters past, nevertheless, before the close of the queen's reign in 1603, two forms of poetry were raised to an excellence never since equalled. The glorious fruitage of the Elizabethan age was in drama and lyric. Much as English poetry may owe to the contributors to *Tottel's Miscellany*, their sonnets and lyrics seem crude indeed beside the matchless verse of the closing years of the century. Equally marked is the difference between the rude comedy and tragedy that England could offer the queen at her coronation and the great plays that were brought for her pleasure from the Bankside to Whitehall before her death. During these few

decades, progress both in lyric and drama was phe-
nomenal. An Elizabethan song-book is filled with
lyrics charming for their simplicity, melody, and
fervor; and the music-lover who looks before and
after thinks unconsciously of "bare ruined choirs
where late the sweet birds sang." In dramatic
literature progress was equally marked; tragedy
responded to all the throbbing emotion and vivid
imagination of the day, and comedy gave its interpretation of life, either beautifully poetic in its
viewpoint or keen and observant in its realism. It
was the age of both lyric and drama.

Although this quick maturing of the Elizabethan
drama remains unparalleled, it is not beyond explanation. For two centuries and more Englishmen had found instruction and diversion in their
plays, till the dramatic instinct was ingrained in
their natures. Into the sacred drama had gone
the highest knowledge and most earnest hope of
those centuries. By long practice the first principles of play-writing and an appreciation of the
art were learned and cultivated. Then came the
Renaissance to quicken the native dramatic impulse. Dramatists were taught to ground their
work firmly on human life; they were furnished
new models and new forms of drama. Instantly,
the crude comedy and tragedy that but yester-
day had sufficed were cast aside; yet, fortunately,
a spiritless imitation of the classical drama was
just as decisively rejected. And the drama sprang
to its great culmination.

It may be harder to explain the rapid development of the Elizabethan lyric. Its perfection, in the first place, lay in form more than in content. At its best, the Elizabethan lyric was marked by spontaneity and fervor, grace and charm, and ease and simplicity of movement. The poets in handling their meters showed a versatility that seems to belie the known facts regarding the newness of this kind of poetry in England. But the poorer lyrics are marred by artificiality and a fondness for strange conceits that betray ingenuity rather than genius in their authors. The song in praise of an imaginary mistress served as a stock theme on which one's skill might be proved. Yet even a reader who knows the worst as well as the best of Elizabethan verse, has one feeling toward the age more strong than any other — that the impulse for song throbbed in the pulse of all England with a force that would inspire poets to the highest achievements in lyric verse.

In other forms of poetry, however, the same power was not shown. Since the Renaissance had brought its vast enrichment to English thought only a few years before, time had not yet elapsed for a full fruition. New meters and a general knowledge of the quantitative principle of verse had been transmitted by the New Learning to the Tudor poets, as well as new forms of poetry like the sonnet and the ode, and new themes in the pastoral and the elegy. At the same time, there was in English hearts enough creative impulse to check the craze for slavish imitation; the Areopagites might theorize on rhythm and exemplify their theories, but Spenser and the inspired English poets had their way. There was impulse, also, sufficient to assimilate much of the artistic acquisition. But in poetry other than drama or lyric the poets were obviously experimenting in a new art. Their classicism was not yet a natural part of their speech; in long efforts their sense of form was not yet sure, for the best in Virgil was but half appreciated. The pastoral, the ode, the elegy, and the epic were left for a later generation to perfect.

Soon the Elizabethan age gave way to the Caroline. The line of demarcation between the two is necessarily shadowy and broken; for the poetry of the one age differed from that of the other not in kind so much as in quality and power. In general, the Caroline authors carried those forms of poetry already perfected on beyond their culmination and down the further slope toward decay. It needs no argument to show that tragedy and comedy became labored and feeble; Brome and Cartwright compare poorly with Jonson and Dekker. It is harder to demonstrate the inferiority of the Caroline lyric. The greatest of the Caroline song writers preserve in part the high traditions they inherited. Carew at his best shows all of Jonson's fine sense of form; Herrick equals the greatest of his predecessors in ease and abandon to lyric impulse. But their work is un-

even in execution, and faults partially nullify the
graces.   Carew is seldom at his best;   Herrick
trifles and has slight sense of values; Donne labors
under a plethora of extraordinary thought.   Fine
as many Caroline lyrics are, even they, like the
drama of the time, show decidedly decadent
tendencies.

Among these Caroline poets Milton is often
called "the last of the Elizabethans," and it is the
purpose of this chapter to justify the designation.
Standing aloof from the prevailing literary influences of his day, Milton contributed nothing to
decadent drama and song.   His contact with the
drama was made rather in the study than in the
playhouse.   Even when he undertook, in one of
his letters, to describe the theatrical repertoire of
Caroline London, his words look back, with only
a passing reference to *Romeo and Juliet* it may be,
to the work of Terence and Seneca.   Ancient literature seemed to him noble and inspiring beside
the low-keyed writings of his contemporaries.   For
this reason, he cared just as little to swell the volume of the love songs.   Leaving that sort of poetry
to "libidinous and ignorant poetasters," as he contemptuously called them, he devoted his talents
to other things, choosing those forms left unde-
veloped by the Elizabethans.   He took from them
the pastoral, the pastoral elegy, the sonnet, and
the masque, and, although he may not have im-
proved in all respects what he attempted, he in-
variably elevated and ennobled what he touched.

In his early years he did not venture upon the longer narrative poem, which he was familiar with in English literature chiefly in Sylvester's translation of Du Bartas, in Daniel's, Drayton's, and Warner's historical poems, and in Spenser's *Faerie Queene*. To accomplish such greater undertakings the schooling of years was necessary; for, although Milton drew inspiration from his immediate predecessors, he had also the wide horizon of the scholar and rose above the standards set by his own generation. In literature as in life his "soul was like a star and dwelt apart."

The secret of Milton's power to ennoble what he attempted lay partly in his character and partly in his training. Where the pastoral and the sonnet depended on classical and Renaissance inspiration, he enjoyed a real advantage. Marlowe had caught instinctively the beauty of classical legend and literature. But the ardor that inspired his impassioned address to Helen of Troy differs widely from the scholarly veneration that Milton had for Grecian poetry. Even far less comparable with Milton's was the scholarship of Gabriel Harvey. He could not have been so stupidly pedantic as he has been represented, although he did actually rank Sylvester on a par with Dante and above Euripides; for he seems to have appreciated the power of much ancient literature.[1] Yet he lacked altogether the creative impulse that Milton possessed, to show him how

[1] Lee, *French Renaissance*, p. 347.

that old art might transform and glorify the new. Milton, however, was scholar and artist combined. He had so thoroughly mastered Latin poetry that not only his Latin verses but also his early English poems show plainly the thorough assimilation of Roman art. He wrote Italian poetry equally well. The fruits of his study, therefore, were knowledge and power combined, and poetic forms that were handled by the Elizabethans with something of unfamiliarity found in Milton a truly sympathetic master.

The relation of the Elizabethans to their new acquisitions from classical antiquity was not dissimilar to the attitude of Milton toward the new scientific discoveries of the seventeenth century. The English humanists had gained a knowledge of a forgotten past as he had come to know the new scientific truth, notably in astronomy. But that truth was still for him and his countrymen in general too strange and too destitute of all but scholarly associations to yield readily to artistic treatment. In the same way, what the Elizabethans had learned of higher creative art was as yet but imperfectly assimilated. It had stimulated their own creative effort, but as artists they still remained in the experimental stage. Milton's scholarship was wide and sure; what he had studied was thoroughly his own; and he handled these exotic types of poetry with both ease and power.

Milton, it has been said, did little for song.

Comus, to be sure, is graced by several charming lyrics, as musical as any in the Elizabethan repertoire. Dr. Burney, indeed, felt that Henry Lawes, who wrote the accompaniments, did them but scant justice. The songs of *Comus*, though, do not represent strictly, either in theme or spirit, the common Elizabethan tradition, and are too few to weigh heavily even in the early work of their author. It is strange that a true musician like Milton, reared in the home of a cultured lover of the art, should have slighted song. His ear, it seems, was attuned to harmony higher than he could find in the Elizabethan song-book or the English psalmody that he loved. It was the music of the Greek chorus and the Pindaric ode that more fully satisfied him. So he turned from the simpler lyric forms of the Elizabethans and with rare artistry composed the elusive music of *Lycidas* and the beautifully modulated verse of *L'Allegro* and *Il Penseroso*.

No type of poetry was more popular among the Elizabethans than the pastoral. One poetical miscellany, *England's Helicon*, was largely filled with it, and all poets gave more or less time to its cultivation; for pastoralism afforded them full opportunity to exercise their powers in new lyric forms and to handle the mythology of antiquity. Of these pastoralists Edmund Spenser was unquestionably the greatest, both in the general pastoral type and in the special form of elegy. His *Shepherd's Calender* and his *Astrophel*, though, im-

press the reader with their artificiality and unreality. Spenser is far less amenable to this blame
than others; for his art is higher than theirs, and
he really has deep-seated convictions to express.
Unfortunately, his thought is seemingly obscured
by his literary convention. He draws pretty pictures of nature and broaches great subjects; but
the garb is so unnatural that it is hard to recognize the true poet beneath it. Much more is this
true of Spenser's contemporaries, and unreality is
the blemish that mars the whole body of Elizabethan pastoralism.

Pastoralism could hardly be other than unreal.
The question of all engrossing interest to these
Tudor poets was whether life in the country or
the city was most free from care. Sidney undoubt-
edly gave the true answer: that he who would
find total exemption from care and trouble must
seek it neither in country nor in city but in the
grave. Yet the literary cult in general shrank from
such brutal truth.[1] Instead, it chose to conjure
up an unreal land, where an idyllic peace might be
enjoyed. In some love lyrics the theme is charm-
ingly developed. Greene's *Shepherd's Wife's Song*,
with its sweetly recurring refrain, pleads for the
shepherd's lot:

> Thus with his wife he spends the year, as blithe
> As doth the king at every tide or sithe;
>   And blither too:
> For kings have wars and broils to take in hand,
> When shepherds laugh and love upon the land.

[1] Courthope, *History of English Poetry*, 2, p. 314.

> Ah then, ah then,
> If country loves such sweet desires do gain,
> What lady would not love a shepherd swain?

The music and delicacy of feeling in such verse gloss over its unreality; but elsewhere, in more strictly pastoral poetry, those saving elements often are lacking.

The unreality of the Elizabethan pastoral is well illustrated by Barnfield. In the conventional way his *Shepheards Content* exalts the rustic's life above the king's. The shepherd

> Sits all Day lowd-piping on a Hill,
> The whilst his flocke about him daunce apace,
> His hart with ioy, his eares with Musique fill:
> Anon a bleating Weather beares the Bace,
> A Lambe the Treble; and to his disgrace
> > Another answers like a middle Meane:
> > Thus euery one to beare a Part are faine.

Elsewhere, Barnfield depicts still more unnaturally the pleasures of the shepherd's life. The poet promises him doves and robins for pets, table delicacies, and fine clothes. It is done with a certain charm in *The Affectionate Shepheard:*

> Wilt thou set springes in a frostie Night,
> To catch the long-bild Woodcocke and the Snype?
> (By the bright glimmering of the Starrie light)
> The Partridge, Phæsant, or the greedie Grype?
> > Ile lend thee lyme-twigs, and fine sparrow calls,
> > Wherewith the Fowler silly Birds inthralls.

But where the charm is greatest the want of deep thought and true emotion is possibly most strongly felt.

Yet from just such pastoral poetry *L'Allegro* and *Il Penseroso* sprang. The reader of Milton can not lose sight of the background of Barnfield's lyrics, if he has ever known them. And even plainer reminiscences of the older poetry may haunt him. The last lines of these two poems bring to mind the close of Marlowe's lyric:

> If these delights thy mind may move,
> Then live with me and be my love,

and the corresponding part of Raleigh's clever rejoinder:

> Then these delights my mind might move
> To live with thee and be thy love.

Or, as one reads of the dawn in *L'Allegro* and the pleasures of the day, the picture in Breton's *Passionate Shepheard* will present itself.[1]

> Who can live in heart so glad
> As the merry country lad?
> Who upon a fair green balk
> May at pleasure sit and walk,
> And amid the azure skies
> See the morning sun arise, —
> While he hears in every spring
> How the birds do chirp and sing:
> Or before the hounds in cry
> See the hare go stealing by:
> Or along the shallow brook,
> Angling with a baited hook,
> See the fishes leap and play
> In a blessèd sunny day:
> Or to hear the partridge call,
> Till she have her covey all:

[1] J. L. Lowes, *Mod. Lang. Rev.*, 6, pp. 206–209.

> Or to see the subtle fox,
> How the villain plies the box:
> After feeding on his prey,
> How he closely sneaks away,
> Through the hedge and down the furrow
> Till he gets into his burrow:
> Then the bee to gather honey,
> And the little black-haired coney,
> On a bank for sunny place,
> With her forefeet wash her face:
> Are not these, with thousands moe
> Than the courts of kings do know,
> The true pleasing spirit's sights
> That may breed true love's delights?

These lines both in content and movement are the most direct forerunners of *L'Allegro*.

But Breton's pastorals in general and one of his little prose works, *Fantastickes*, are written in this same idyllic vein. *Fantastickes* consists of a series of neat little prose essays, resembling somewhat the sketches of the character books, on the different seasons of the year, the twelve months, and the twelve hours of the day. In these the reader is reminded of *L'Allegro*. At "three of the clocke" "the Cocke cals the seruants to their dayes work, . . . the Milke-maids begin to looke toward their dayry, . . . the Sparrow beginnes to chirpe about the house." At four o'clock, "crowes the Cocke lustily, and claps his wings for ioy of the light, and with his Hennes leaps lightly from his Roust." At five, "the Maids are at milking, and the seruants at Plough; . . . the Shepheard is almost gotten to his Fold; . . . the hounds begin to find after the Hare, and horse and foot follow after the cry." At six, "the Mower falles to whetting of his Sythe, and the Beaters of Hempe giue a hoh to euery blow." And so through the series of little sketches, the reader comes upon one reminder after another of the chosen pleasures of L'Allegro's day.

It is interesting to see how Milton has retouched this background with an artist's hand. The besetting sin of the Elizabethan poet was his proneness to indulge in strange conceits or excesses of fancy. Barnfield, for example, in support of the oft-expressed preference for black to white, presents a long series of illustrations drawn from animate and inanimate nature. Of this ingenious argument, which was carried on even by Sidney and Shakespeare in their sonnets, only a faint reminiscence appears in the lines of *Il Penseroso:*

> Black, but such as in esteem
> Prince Memnon's sister might beseem.

Barnfield is unable to go far without indulgence in such conceit. He can prove that a shepherd is courtier, scholar, soldier, and gentleman, and then end his argument with the assertion:

> In whose sweete lap Ile lay me downe to sleepe,
> And neuer wake till Marble-stones shall weepe.

But Milton, even in his early poems, seldom yields to this craze for novelty, and he follows consistently the highway of poetic art.

L'Allegro and *Il Penseroso*, therefore, are written

with an art that exalts them far above the pastoral type. The classicism that graces them betokens the poet as well as the scholar; it shows, in addition to learning, an imaginative reworking of old legend. The little glimpses that the poems give of natural scenery are as real as they are charming. The cottage half hidden by the oaks, the little window fringed with creepers, the hedgerow elms, the mountains and the shore, and the nightingale among the trees — all are there. The efforts of readers to identify the locality give proof of the poet's truth to nature. But something more than this lends a reality to *L'Allegro* and *Il Penseroso* that the Elizabethan pastoral never possessed. Instead of the fanciful pleasures of an unreal existence, Milton here describes the true delights of a man of taste and sensibility and the real pastimes of rural England. Such a man in his more carefree moods finds in nature's stirring life a real appeal and in rustic society a true companionship. During moods of reflection he can find amid these same natural surroundings an equal charm and inspiration, and from the world of books and music a stimulus to which even in his other mood he was not unresponsive. Thus Milton has interpreted nature from the true standpoint of mood; he has associated man with the world in which he lives. Pastoralism, which remains in the poems only as a background, thus yields place to a true interpretation of life.

In respect to form, also, these two poems carry

higher the Elizabethan pastoral. The Tudor lyrist possessed sure artistry only in comparatively short songs, and in simple, though melodious and ever-varying, verse and stanza forms. Far higher is the art of Milton. The subtle musical cadences left by the rhythm, as it accommodates itself freely to the most delicate changes in thought or sound, show the master musician. Here is literary art working in minutiæ. Equally striking is the artistic structure of the poems. Milton set the same pattern for the development of the two moods. *L'Allegro* begins by banishing melancholy, as a mood inharmonious with his feelings; *Il Penseroso* begins with the banishment of vain, deluding joys. Each poem, with the same employment of classical imagery and allusion, after invoking companions suited to its mood, passes on to a description of its sense of true delight. How close the correspondence really is between the two, only a careful scrutiny can reveal. A single line, for example, in one, "so buxom, blithe, and debonair," finds its close counterpart in the other's, "sober, steadfast, and demure." Clearly, Milton is developing with an artist's hand a carefully wrought plan. In each case he works with the surest grasp of total effect. Both poems rise forcefully from their beautiful beginnings to fine artistic climaxes; for the music of the lines and the beauty of the thought seem to increase as they approach their ends. It is often said that the close of *Il Penseroso* represents the high water

LIBRARY
College of St. Francis
JOLIET, ILL.

44228

mark of English poetry. In form the two poems are unrivalled.

It would be needless to comment on the exquisite phrasing of these companion poems. Here is all the old Elizabethan facility of expression, with something of conscious art added in place of the old-time spontaneity; but the aptly chosen adjectives and the compact phrases, that suggest pictures rich in color, sound, and movement and modulate the verses sweetly to the ear, can not be described.

Even more conspicuous is the excellence of *Lycidas* as compared with the pastoral elegies of the Tudor period. Its thought, like theirs, is expressed in the conventional language of elegy. King is spoken of as a poet-shepherd, with whom his bosom friend, the author of the lament, was wont to perform the idealized duties of their calling and sing their rustic songs. Nature, too, mourns for King as it commonly has done since the lament for Bion was written. Because of such adherence to convention *Lycidas* was severely arraigned by truth-loving Dr. Johnson. This, he asserted, is not the language of sincere grief; for grief has no leisure or inclination for fiction. What a truthful elegy should be his own poem on Dr. Levet shows.

> Well try'd, through many a varying year,
> See Levet to the grave descend,
> Officious, innocent, sincere,
> Of ev'ry friendless name the friend.

> Yet still he fills affection's eye
> Obscurely wise, and coarsely kind;
> Nor, letter'd arrogance, deny
> Thy praise to merit unrefined.

In these words Johnson frankly admits his friend's obscurity and uncouthness, never thinking that concealment would honor the memory of the great-hearted man. This is Grecian directness in facing the facts of life. Nevertheless, conventionality in expression is not necessarily a proof of insincerity, and a truthful poet or sculptor can employ conventional modes of expression for even the deepest thought.

Another objection raised against *Lycidas* has been that no Christian poet can truly combine, as Milton does, the pagan and the Christian religions. But such incongruity is characteristic of all Milton's poetry. The note of regret that is heard in the *Ode on the Morning of Christ's Nativity*, a regret for the passing of the old pagan mythology, indicates that Milton saw in it an expression of some enduring truths and beauties of life. So in *Lycidas* he could truthfully speak of Jove's just appraisal of all human endeavor, for the name signified to Milton poetically the Christian God. Throughout, the poem expresses Christian truths by pagan symbols, and there is no impropriety in Milton's changing to a literal expression of his faith in the closing lines.

Neither the Elizabethan elegy nor *Lycidas*, therefore, can be branded insincere merely because it employs a poet's language. The older type of elegy, however, sounds insincere because its thought is more shallow, its employment of classical allusion less easy, and its whole manner more conscious than the thought and manner of *Lycidas*. Milton's art is sure enough of itself to take the elegiac convention and beautify it. The universal mourning of nature, the description of the flowers, the procession of mourners, and all other elegiac traditions are beautifully interwoven to adorn the great truth that mankind has need of such high-minded idealists as King seemed to Milton to have been. The separate portions of *Lycidas* articulate perfectly. The poet's thoughts on self at the beginning, the reference to the earnest student's life at Cambridge, the meditation on fame, and even the censure of the selfish clergy, all harmonize and lead artistically to the words of Christian consolation at the close. Then come the poet's own simple words after the shepherd's monody is done. These lines have been often interpreted as a reference on Milton's part to his plans for future composition. It is far better to take them in a larger way. The tribute to the dead has been paid; the time for mourning is past; and now before the poet lies the future, large in its possibilities and its hope. From the bitter loss a richer sense of life has come, as it came to Tennyson in *In Memoriam*.

A relationship between *Lycidas* and its Elizabethan prototypes, especially Spenser's pastorals, can here and there be traced. Milton's fine description of the flowers grew from these lines in the *Shepherd's Calender:*

> Bring hether the Pincke and purple Cullambine,
> With Gelliflowres;
> Bring Coronations, and Sops in wine,
>   Worne of Paramoures:
> Strowe me the ground with Daffadowndillies,
> And Cowslips, and Kingcups, and loued Lillies:
>   The pretie Pawnce,
>   And the Cheuisaunce,
> Shall match with the fayre flowre Delice.

There are portions of Spenser's poems, too, that recall Milton's attack on the clergy. Piers condemns those shepherds [clergymen] "that playen while their flockes be unfedde," and those others who

> Caren as little as they
> What fallen the flocke, so they han the fleece,
> And get all the gayne, paying but a peece.

Even Milton's celebrated digression on fame looks back to Spenser's lines:

> Cuddie, the prayse is better then the price,
> The glory eke much greater than the gayne.

In addition, there are many similarities in detail between *Lycidas* and the *Shepherd's Calender*, of which the reference to St. Michael's Mount is typical.[1] Clearly, Spenser and the Elizabethan elegiac poets had added their quota to Milton's knowledge of this classical poetic form.

[1] See *S's. C.*, "April," ll. 136–144; "May," ll. 37–48; "July," ll. 165–168; "October," ll. 19–20; "July," l. 41.

But *Lycidas* shows only these faint and incidental reminders of older English elegies; for, although Milton knew them, he as usual sought not the most accessible but the best models. He therefore turned to Theocritus, Virgil, and some of the Italian poets for guidance. In Theocritus he found both the fundamental conception of pastoral poetry and sincerity and naturalness of expression; from Moschus he copied the fiction of the literary ties that had drawn the mourner and his dead friend together; from Virgil he learned how firm the pastoral's structure may be; and from the Italian poets he derived authority for the introduction of satire and protest in the midst of his lament. Lastly, he added the best that English poetry had to contribute to the enrichment of the elegy. *Lycidas*, in short, is a rich composite of all the best that literature had to offer; yet the debt on Milton's part was really unconscious, so thoroughly imbued was his mind with his wide reading in the world's literature. No finer instance than *Lycidas* can be found of the artist's true receptivity.

The sonnets of Shakespeare's time bear an even less direct relation than the elegies to Milton's work. The Elizabethan sonneteers, taking the universally accepted themes of the Italian poets, gave them vogue in England. It was expression and not thought that Tudor poets valued, and many of the best of their efforts were virtually translations. Daniel's "Care-charmer

Sleep, son of the sable Night," is only a close rendering of one of Desportes' best sonnets. These English poets, however, who pilfered Italian and French literatures so boldly, possessed a style of their own and devised a new form of sonnet that allowed them more fluency and ease in expression. Their work is often trivial in thought and over fanciful in language; its charm is fluency, a rare beauty in occasional pictures, and a profundity revealed in scattered reflections on life. In the last, especially, Shakespeare surpassed all others. Milton, however, designed his sonnets to serve his highest thought and most personal feeling. Hence he went back, as he had done in *Lycidas*, to models more remote than those of Elizabethan England. He preferred the Italian form of sonnet, apparently for its greater dignity and power, and except in two or three lighter pieces, like that on the nightingale, he confined himself in the sonnets to serious reflections on self and the great occurrences of the time. His form of expression may be no higher than the Elizabethans' at their best; but his mood is more exalted and his purposes more serious. Landor's judgment seems adequate and fair, that Milton

> Caught the sonnet from the dainty hand
> Of Love, who cried to lose it, and he gave
> The notes to glory.

Still another form of literature was carried by Milton to a higher level than had been reached by his predecessors. There are sticklers for form who maintain that *Comus* is simply a lyric drama and not a masque, because it does not conform strictly to the type as students define it. These critics allege that the actors in *Comus*, besides speaking their parts, carry through the elaborate dances, since no special masquers are provided for. The plot of *Comus*, also, is something more than an excuse for the music and the scenic display. These, to be sure, are notable departures from the Jacobean type of masque, in which the plot was slight and the actors who handled the plot and the masquers who performed the elaborate fixed dances and processionals formed two distinct groups. But Milton himself in his own manuscript and his first editor as well, call the poem a masque. And, indeed, there are in *Comus* many resemblances to this dramatic type.[1] Its charming use of old legend and of classical mythology; its beautiful songs; its two anti-masques, one at the beginning, where the anti-masque usually came, of Comus's rout, the other of the rustics at the close; and the idealized pictures of rural life, all accord strictly with the treatment of the Jacobean poets. To refuse *Comus* the designation that its author gave it, seems mere pedantry.

In *Comus* Milton, as usual, has simply adapted his pattern to suit his occasion and his own peculiar temperament. Naturally wishing to please the Earl of Bridgewater and his family, the author added to the importance of the chil-

[1] See Reyher, *Les Masques Anglais*, pp. 212–216.

dren's parts by assigning them the masques as
well as the dialogue. The masque in Milton's
early manhood was still a living dramatic form,
and, like any other living organism, was rightly
subject to modifications like these. His temperament, also, as well as his occasion, dictated a departure from the Jacobean type. Milton was not
content that his piece should be simply a grace-
ful compliment to a noble family and a charming
bit of fancy for an evening's entertainment. He
wished it to convey his own high thoughts on
serious matters — his own ideals of life. *Comus*,
therefore, becomes a poetic homily on temperance
in its broadest sense. Jonson had aimed at instruction in some of his masques, but he did not
key them so high as did Milton. The beauty of
temperate living and the power of righteousness
to defeat evil, are the texts of this arch-idealist in
Comus. The author presents his ideal in two
ways — by making vice repulsive and virtue attractive; and he leaves with the reader the highest sense of moral elevation. With no loss of
beauty the masque was thus dignified and exalted
by the Puritan poet.

The sources of *Comus* are of especial interest in
this connection, because they are mainly of the
Elizabethan period. Of course, Homer's *Odyssey*
is Milton's ultimate original; but all the most
essential features of his masque can be traced to
works of the sixteenth or seventeenth centuries
that he must have known. The union of the stories

of Circe and Comus, which in Homer are quite separate, was made by Henry du Puy, in a Latin work, *Comus, sive Phagesiposia Cimmeria,* which was written in 1608 and was in circulation in England before the composition of Milton's poem.[1] The germ of Milton's plot, also, the search of two brothers for a sister who has been charmed by a wicked sorcerer, is to be found in a sixteenth-century source, Peele's *Old Wives Tale,* that strangest of Pre-Shakespearean plays. The charming songs of *Comus,* furthermore, take one back irresistibly to Fletcher's *Faithful Shepherdess,* although the moral tone of the two works is entirely different. For the moral spirit of Milton's masque one must turn to Jonson's *Pleasure Reconciled to Virtue,* where Hercules and twelve gentleman masquers uphold temperance and virtue against the bestial excesses of Comus, "the god of cheer, or the Belly." In William Browne's *Inner Temple Masque,* a story of Circe and Ulysses, the anti-masque, as in *Comus,* is made up of men who have been transformed by Circe into monsters. Finally, in Spenser's *Faerie Queene* Milton found the Bower of Bliss, where the knight Guyon overthrows Acrasia and rescues men enslaved in her brutish train. The freeing of Amoret, too, from the spells of the enchanter resembles the corresponding incident in *Comus,* which in general preserves the old machinery of the romance, as it was found in Tasso and Spenser.

[1] See Stern, I, pp. 229–230 for an outline of this work.

So Milton took these four forms of poetry, the pastoral, the elegy, the sonnet, and the masque, an imperfect inheritance from the Elizabethan age, and raised them to an excellence they never before had reached. At the same time, he was meditating some great achievement in poetry that should distinguish and ennoble English literature as the epics of Homer, Virgil, and Dante had ennobled the literatures of their native lands. For this vast undertaking Milton had still less satisfactory models in English sources. Elizabethan poets had attempted the long historical poem, such as *Albion's England* and *The Civil Wars of York and Lancaster*. Giles Fletcher, Sylvester, and, above all others, Spenser furnished other specimens of the long poem, which were of influence on Milton's epic. But although Meres called Daniel the Homer and Drayton the Virgil of England, no one of these poets could set Milton a pattern in artistic structure. His epics, therefore, are less dependent on earlier English literature than are his minor poems, and it is in them that he proves his claim to the designation, "the last of the Elizabethans."

This phrase, however, should be used with proper reservations. Milton belonged only in part to the Elizabethan age. Born twenty years after the defeat of the Spanish Armada, and five years after the death of the queen herself, he lived through the stirring Puritan epoch and on into the dark days of the Restoration. Even in his earliest poetry, therefore, he could not be an Elizabethan pure and simple, for the Puritan influence had already affected him strongly. This new force soon dominated his life and molded his character, so that when he composed his great epics he seems to have outlived the Elizabethan traits of his youth. New forces had transformed his thoughts, and a new theme and a new form of poetry demanded other modes of expression. Yet Milton was even more removed from the Restoration age, in which he then wrote, than from the Elizabethan. Dryden is the great exponent of that new era, and how different his spirit and his poetry from Milton's. Even in his epics Milton is closer kin to the Elizabethans than to the wits of the new era. His fine choice of phrase, his powerful creative imagination, and his love for the poetry rather than the facts of life, link him with the old Elizabethan age. Puritanism had not stamped out the inborn poetic spirit, and among the poets of the new era he stands as "the last of the Elizabethans."

Chapter II

Milton's Temperament and Ideals

MILTON'S relation, however, either to Elizabethan or Puritan England can not be understood without an intimate acquaintance with his temperament and ideals. No finer instance of conscientious, unswerving loyalty to an ideal can anywhere be found than in the life of Milton. The fine sonnet composed on his twenty-third birthday is not his earliest expressed recognition of a divine call to high service, nor are the noble words of the *Second Defence* his last. He there asserts: "I never, at any time, wrote anything which I did not think agreeable to truth, to justice, and to piety"; and the proud boast is reaffirmed in the lines of *Paradise Lost:*

> More safe I sing with mortal voice, unchanged
> To hoarse or mute, though fallen on evil days,
> On evil days though fallen, and evil tongues,
> In darkness, and with dangers compassed round,
> And solitude.

From beginning to end Milton pursued the same high ideals. As distinctly as the prophet Isaiah, he had seen the vision of human lips touched by divinely illumined coals of fire, of a human life set apart from and above the mass of humanity;

in the genuineness of his high calling he never lost confidence.

Just how much of his prophetic impulse Milton owed to his father can never be known. He gratefully acknowledges in *Ad Patrem:*

> Thou never bad'st me tread
> The beaten path and broad that leads right on
> To opulence, nor didst condemn thy son
> To the insipid clamours of the bar,
> To laws voluminous and ill observed;
> But, wishing to enrich me more, to fill
> My mind with treasure, ledst me far away
> From city din to deep retreats, to banks
> And streams Aonian, and, with free consent,
> Didst place me happy at Apollo's side.[1]

In these words Milton bears testimony to the aspirations of his father to something higher than material success for his son. This same sort of parental encouragement and assistance laid the foundations for the stimulating criticism of John Ruskin and the virile poetry of Robert Browning. Had Milton had another home environment, the course of his life might have been very different from what it was.

Milton, it is true, soon felt compelled to disregard the more specific wishes of his parent. In the seventeenth century the church still offered for scholars and literary men the most lucrative offices and the most attractive vocation, and toward the church Milton in his youth almost inevitably turned. The choice was made, he tells

[1] Quoted from Corson, *Introduction to Milton*, p. 38.

us, both "by the intentions of my parents and friends . . . and in mine own resolutions."[1] But "coming to some maturity of years," he continues, "and perceiving what tyranny had invaded the church, that he who would take orders must subscribe slave, . . . I thought it better to prefer a blameless silence before the sacred office of speaking, bought and begun with servitude and forswearing." The decision to abandon the sacred calling was reached not without some opposition from the father; *Ad Patrem* seems as much an apology for disregard of parental wishes as an elaborate compliment and expression of gratitude. He reminds his parent that "verse is a work divine," and that it, as well as the ministry, brings to its devotees true uplift. The implication of his words is plain: better whole-hearted service of the muses than selfish adherence to a tyrannical ecclesiastical organization.

Abandonment of his first high intentions did not mean for Milton a lowering, or even an alteration, of his ideals. Literature and scholarship, as he pursued them, brought him into kinship with all who have followed a lofty purpose in any walk of life. It may well be of himself that he is thinking in *Samson Agonistes* when he writes:

> Why was my breeding ordered and prescribed
> As of a person separate to God,
> Designed for great exploits, if I must die
> Betrayed, captived, and both my eyes put out.

[1] *Ch. Gov.*, 2, p. 482.

Possibly a similar interpretation is permissible of Christ's words in *Paradise Regained:*

> When I was yet a child, no childish play
> To me was pleasing; all my mind was set
> Serious to learn and know, and thence to do,
> What might be public good; myself I thought
> Born to that end, born to promote all truth,
> All righteous things.

When these aspirations first exerted their influence, Milton seemed pre-eminently a child of the Renaissance; intense seriousness, like his, in the pursuit of an ideal was as possible for a Greek as for a Puritan. From boyhood Milton had felt strongly the appeal of the beautiful. In a letter to his closest friend he wrote in 1637:

What besides God has resolved concerning me I know not, but this at least: He has instilled into me, if into any one, a vehement love of the beautiful. Not with so much labour, as the fables have it, is Ceres said to have sought her daughter, Proserpina, as it is my habit day and night to seek for this idea of the beautiful, as for a certain image of supreme beauty, through all the forms and faces of things (for many are the shapes of things divine). — Hence it is that, when any one scorns what the vulgar opine in their depraved estimation of things, and dares to feel and speak and be that which the highest wisdom throughout all ages has taught to be best, to that man I attach myself forthwith by a kind of real necessity, wherever I find him.[1]

[1] To Charles Diodati, Letter 7 (1637).

In this interesting self-examination Milton not only proclaims his allegiance to the beautiful — "what the highest wisdom throughout all ages has taught to be best" — but also his conviction that this divine spirit is to be found embodied in many forms. This is the attitude of the Renaissance, not of medievalism or Puritanism, toward life — a full realization of all its manifold possibilities. The youthful poet, then, was at this time the child of the Renaissance.

With this for his impelling ideal, Milton willingly submitted, even in his earliest school-days, to the most rigid intellectual discipline. All that the literatures of Greece and Rome contain, and all that France and Italy could offer, were placed at his disposal by the generosity of his father. To these subjects Milton added the study of music, mathematics, and the other sciences, and finally illuminated all this learning by converse with cultured friends and well-advised travel in France and Italy. Everywhere his remarkable powers and worth were recognized — at Cambridge, as his own words testify; in the household of Sir Henry Wotton; and among the *literati* of Italy. Regarding the trivial interests of life Milton speaks less often, possibly because his autobiographical confessions are usually prompted by grave thoughts and serious emergencies. Chance references in his letters to Diodati, however, as well as the general spirit of *L'Allegro*, show that he had sympathy with the pleasures as well as the duties of men.

During his university days he visited the theaters of London, roamed abroad to enjoy the beauties of suburban scenery, and shared in the innocent diversions of the country folk. It is, then, a mistake to regard him as a person devoid of ordinary human interests and passions. But it is true that his complete absorption in the pursuits of the Renaissance, as well as the intensity of his devotion to the Puritan ideal, gradually broke these points of contact with the lighter sides of life. In a college letter, for example, written to his former teacher, Alexander Gill, he complained that at Cambridge he found too few serious-minded men. And in the *Epitaphium Damonis* he alludes with real pathos to the loneliness of the human heart. His main concern was the cultivation of mind and character.

Milton's love of the English countryside, however, is one of the quiet pleasures that apparently never left him. He wrote as a youth to Diodati of his excursions into the country, and in *L'Allegro* he drew his beautiful picture of the pleasures of rural life. The glimpses which are there given of the thatched cottages, the hedge-rows of the quiet lanes, and the cheery sounds coming from the country people at their work or play, are as real as they are sympathetic. How fixed these pictures were in the poet's memory one may infer from the vivid recollections cherished of them in his blindness. In *Paradise Lost* there occurs this echo of *L'Allegro:*

As one who, long in populous city pent,
Where houses thick and sewers annoy the air,
Forth issuing on a summer's morn, to breathe
Among the pleasant villages and farms
Adjoined, from each thing met conceives delight —
The smell of grain, of tedded grass, or kine,
Or dairy, each rural sight, each rural sound —
If chance with nymph-like step fair virgin pass,
What pleasing seemed for her now pleases more,
She most, and in her look sums all delight.[1]

Only force of circumstances kept this phase of Milton's temperament in the background, and the same can be assumed of other lighter interests natural to him.

Side by side with this liberal humanism there developed in Milton a severe, though cultured, Puritanism. Would one be a poet? Then "let him live sparely, after the manner of the Samian master; let herbs afford him his innocent diet, let clear water in a beechen cup stand near him, and let him drink sober draughts from a pure fountain!" [2] "Nothing," he likewise declared before his university associates, "can deservedly be taken into account as among the causes of our happiness that does not somehow or other regard both that everlasting life and this civil life below." [3] Such serious recognition of life's grave responsibilities marks the poet's whole career; the *Sonnet on his having arrived at the age of Twenty-three* is as characteristic of him as the *Ode on a Grecian Urn* is of Keats. In consequence, Milton as poet as-

---

[1] *P. L.*, 9, ll. 445–454.   [2] *Elegia Sexta.*   [3] *Prolusion*, 6.

pired to something higher than superficial imitation of the graces of English humanism —

> Those new-fangled toys, and trimming slight
> Which takes our late fantastics with delight.

With higher visions for the poet he wrote, apostrophizing the language:

> Yet I had rather, if I were to choose,
> Thy service in some graver subject use,
> Such as may make thee search thy coffers round,
> Before thou clothe my fancy in fit sound:
> Such where the deep transported mind may soar
> Above the wheeling poles, and at Heaven's door
> Look in, and see each blissful deity.[1]

This is simply the youthful humanist's way of expressing his high Puritan aspirations.

Such a combination of these diverse attitudes toward life is quite in accord with the higher trend taken by the Revival of Learning in England. The movement in Italy was dominated entirely by æsthetic impulses, and letters and the arts flourished at the expense of morality. But in England the interests of the New Learning were controlled by the nation's ethical ideals, and the new studies were passionately pursued for what they could yield to England's uplift. Erasmus, for example, working in the service of the church, prepared his scholarly edition of the *Greek Testament*, while More, in the interests of society and humanity, dreamed his *Utopia*. In the same spirit, John Colet, the founder of St. Paul's School,

[1] *Vacation Exercise*, ll. 19-20, 29-35.

placed over the master's chair in the school-room the picture of Christ and the motto, "Hear ye him." Even Colet, however, could not have demanded a more whole-hearted obedience to this injunction than Milton's, who was once a pupil at St. Paul's. He was humanistic enough in temperament to agree with those Greek philosophers who taught that virtue without knowledge is impossible. But in subscribing to this tenet he would also insist on its converse, that knowledge without virtue is of no avail. His whole attitude toward life was determined by the close mingling of the two supposedly antithetic movements, Puritanism and humanism.

In some of Milton's works one side of his nature is more in evidence, in other parts the other side; but *Paradise Lost* seems to be the harmonious blending, in about equal degrees, of both humanism and Puritanism. This statement may seem at variance with commonly accepted opinion. The majority of its readers have appreciated only the Biblical origin of *Paradise Lost* and its religious and theological trend. They have read it as a faithful recital of historical fact, and indeed have accepted its version of Lucifer's revolt and Adam's fall as canonical. But *Paradise Lost* represents, also, the fruits of Milton's close study of classical literature and the critical and creative writings of the Italian Renaissance. He had before him not simply the *Iliad*, the *Odyssey*, and the *Aeneid*, but *Jerusalem Delivered* and the whole body of Italian

criticism.   From all that was of high merit in
secular literature, as well as from the *Bible*, Milton
derived his inspiration.

The poet's hope was to achieve some enduring
monument for English letters.   To attain this high
ideal no artist ever submitted to longer or more
rigorous training.   The position he might easily
have won among Cavalier song writers did not
attract him.   Even his efforts at Horton, fine as
they were in sentiment, and rich as they were in
subtle musical harmonies and in finely suggestive
pictures, failed to satisfy.   Hence Milton did not
hasten to publish those early poems, which were
not printed by him till 1645.   Something far
grander in proportions and more majestic in theme
had become his ambition.   To achieve this the
poet resigned hope of immediate fame and worked
for a distant reward.

The fruition of his labors was destined to be
remote.   Milton worked slowly, being possibly, as
he admits, "by nature slow and lazy to write."
The manuscript copy of his early poems attests
in its numerous corrections his scrupulous care.
His whole energy, moreover, was soon absorbed
by other duties.   But, even in the most busy days
of the Latin secretaryship, his thoughts still centered on the one great goal.   Of his absorption
in scholarship at this time his nephew, Edward
Phillips, gives an interesting picture: "Here he
liv'd a private and quiet life, still prosecuting his
studies and curious search into knowledge, the

grand affair perpetually of his life." Milton himself could truly say, "an idle ease has never had charms for me"; and he never lost hope "that by labour and intense study (which I take to be my portion in this life), joined with the strong propensity of nature, I might perhaps leave something so written to aftertimes, as they should not willingly let die." [1]

Whatever came to hinder him in his chosen study was regarded as an interruption, for Milton felt himself "led by the genial power of nature to another task." "O perfect and accomplish thy glorious acts," he beseeches Christ, "for men may leave their works unfinished, but thou art a God, thy nature is perfection. . . . And he that now for haste snatches up a plain, ungarnished present as a thank-offering to thee, . . . may then perhaps take up a harp, and sing thee an elaborate song to generations." [2] Only for the service of the Commonwealth was he content "to interrupt the pursuit of no less hopes than these." And in so doing he by no means forgot "the thing which I had to say, and those intentions which have lived within me ever since I could conceive myself worth anything to my country." Still seeing in vision, then, as he had dreamed in youth, Milton could exclaim: "Neither do I think it shame to covenant with any knowing reader, that for some few years yet I may go on trust with him

[1] *Familiar Letters, 14; Ch. Gov.*, 2, p. 477.
[2] *Animadversions*, 3, p. 72.

toward the payment of what I am now indebted, as being a work not to be raised from the heat of youth, or the vapours of wine; . . . but by devout prayer to that eternal Spirit, who can enrich with all utterance and knowledge, and sends out his seraphim, with the hallowed fire of his altar, to touch and purify the lips of whom he pleases. . . . I trust hereby to make it manifest with what small willingness I endure to interrupt the pursuit of no less hopes than these, and leave a calm and pleasing solitariness, fed with cheerful and confident thoughts, to embark in a troubled sea of noises and hoarse disputes, put from beholding the bright countenance of truth in the quiet and still air of delightful studies, to come into the dim reflection of hollow antiquities sold by the seeming bulk." [1]

For the highest, most exalted literary expression to which Milton thus aspired, there were two models or types, the epic and tragedy, fully sanctioned by the use and theory of antiquity and the Renaissance. Other forms of poetry — the pastoral drama of the Song of Solomon, as Milton terms it, the odes of Pindar, the lyrics of the Prophets — might suffice for other themes; but Milton approved only of these two for what he had to express. Of the two, the epic unquestionably enjoyed the preference of Renaissance humanists. The drama of the Greeks had lain so long virtually unknown, and the authority of Virgil was so supreme during all the Middle Ages, that the epic

[1] *Ch. Gov.*, 2, pp. 480–481.

was usually preferred over tragedy. It may seem strange, therefore, that Milton should have first considered tragedy for his purpose. But since his reason for this, as well as his motives for deciding ultimately in favor of the epic, were dictated by the theme selected, further consideration of the matter must be for the time postponed.

To the selection of his theme Milton gave the most earnest thought. Moved by the example of Dante and the Italian epic poets, as well as by his own patriotic impulse, he aspired not simply to become the "interpreter and relater of the best and sagest things," but also to "fix all the industry and art" he possessed "to the adorning of my native tongue." [1] Some advantages would have been gained by the use of Latin as the medium of expression, but they were not sufficient to offset his preference for English. The selection of a theme, however, was no such easy matter. He first decided that the poem should be based on some incident in early British history and have enduring significance for Englishmen. To this determination he was led by the example of other epic poets, who in general have treated matters derived from the histories of their own countries. Homer tells of the war of Greece against Troy and the wanderings of the great Odysseus; Virgil recounts the establishment of the Roman race in Italy; Tasso celebrates mainly the heroism of Italian knighthood. The first step,

[1] *Ch. Gov.*, 2, p. 478.

then, in the growth of Milton's epic was his decision to narrate in the mother tongue some incident from British history.

To be sure, in the *Vacation Exercise* he had expressed a desire to deal with heavenly things, and in the great *Ode*, written shortly after, he had realized the wish with unquestioned success. But he had felt obliged to leave *The Passion* unfinished, on finding "this subject . . . to be above the years he had." For his large undertaking his thoughts were first directed to British history. In a letter to Mansus he alludes to the plan in these words: "If perchance I shall ever call back into verse our native kings, and Arthur stirring war even under the earth that hides him, or speak of the great-souled heroes, the knights of the unconquered Table." This project is next enlarged upon in the *Epitaphium Damonis*:

> I have a theme of the Trojans cruising our southern headlands
> Shaping to song, and the realm of Imogen, daughter of Pandras,
> Brennus and Arvirach, dukes, and Bren's bold brother, Belinus;
> Then the Armorican settlers under the laws of the Britons,
> Ay, and the womb of Igraine fatally pregnant with Arthur,
> Uther's son, whom he got disguised in Gorlois' likeness,
> All by Merlin's craft. . . .
>   Prize sufficiently ample
> Mine, and distinction great (unheard of ever thereafter
> Though I should be, and inglorious, all through the world of the
>   stranger),
> If but yellow-haired Ouse shall read me, the drinker of Alan,
> Humber, which whirls as it flows, and Trent's whole valley of orchards,
> Thames, my own Thames, above all, and Tamar's western waters,
> Tawny with ores, and where the white waves swinge the far Orkneys.[1]

[1] Translation by Masson.

But Milton was equally determined that this British story should be Christian, not pagan, in sentiment. He aspired: "To sing victorious agonies of martyrs and saints, the deeds and triumphs of just and pious nations, doing valiantly through faith against the enemies of Christ; to deplore the general relapses of kingdoms and states from justice and God's true worship. Lastly, whatsoever in religion is holy and sublime, in virtue amiable or grave, whatsoever hath passion or admiration, . . . all these things with a solid and treatable smoothness to paint out and describe." [1] Such confidence in the Christian religion to supply heroic themes for the modern poet had been previously expressed by Minturno and Tasso, to whom Milton a moment later alludes. Italian critics were agreed that the true hero for the modern epic must be not alone mighty in combat but also true in faith. Hence came Milton's second determination — to exhibit the "pattern of a Christian hero."

But if the theme of the great poem was to be Christian, why could it not be sought in sacred history as well as in British legend? The story of the Hebrew people was still regarded as the type of universal history, revealing God's ways not simply toward the chosen people but toward all mankind, and bearing therefore for the English a really national significance. In the *Bible*, furthermore, Milton found the best models of

[1] *Ch. Gov.*, 2, p. 479.

literature; "the Scripture," he continues, "also
affords us a divine pastoral drama in the Song of
Solomon. . . . And the Apocalypse of St. John is
the majestic image of a high and stately tragedy."
Surely, then, sacred story might easily be adapted
to literary treatment; it was as germane to modern English life as British history, and as inspiring
artistically as any secular theme could be. So,
long before *Paradise Lost* was begun, Milton was
turning over in his mind the suitability of various
themes. About the year 1640 he drew up a list of
the subjects then under consideration. There are
in all about one hundred titles, all designed, it
seems, for tragedy. Only thirty-three of these
entries relate to British history, and not one, it
is interesting to note, concerns King Arthur. Sixty
titles designate Biblical stories, of which only eight
are from the *New Testament*. The stories of
Adam, Abraham, Sodom, and John the Baptist
were among those on the list. In most cases
nothing beyond the mere title was suggested, for
as yet Milton had approached no decision; but
even the bare list shows the growing inclination
of the poet to handle a scriptural theme.[1]

Of all the stories from the *Bible* brought under
consideration, one especially seemed to possess to
full degree the heroism, the Christian principle,
and the vital relation to national life and experi-

[1] Following the growth of Milton's plans in this way, one is able
to appreciate the full significance of the lines at the beginning of the
ninth book of *Paradise Lost*.

ence that the great poem, according to the teaching of the humanists, must embrace. The story of Adam might easily be taken to represent the history of the whole race. According to the old theology, mankind owes to Adam not simply its existence, but its destiny as well; for Adam bequeathed first life to man, then sin, and, lastly, the means of ultimate salvation. Hence this story clearly held preference in Milton's mind as he considered his plans. Instead of simply listing it among the titles jotted down, Milton sketches more or less fully four separate drafts for a tragedy based upon the story of Eden. Hugo Grotius, whom Milton had met in Paris in 1638, had published, over thirty years before, a drama, *Adamus Exsul*, and Giovanni Battista Andreini in 1613 had produced his version, *L'Adamo*. Vondel's *Lucifer* appeared in 1654. Other poets, it is true, had given non-dramatic form to at least portions of the story. But scholars of the seventeenth century highly esteemed tragedy constructed after classical models, and naturally Milton, despite the preference of the Renaissance for the epic, followed the literary taste of the day. Thus his choice of theme and his apparent preference for tragedy can be explained.

The first two drafts for the tragedy on Adam which the Cambridge manuscript contains, give mere lists of the intended *dramatis personæ*, most of whom are allegorical abstractions such as Conscience, Labour, Ignorance, and Death. With

such characters the drama could scarcely have
been carried through, and Milton rejected both
drafts as unsatisfactory. The third draft is
considerably more energized. Act III, besides
relating the fall of Lucifer, presents the fallen
angel himself "contriving Adam's ruin." In
Act IV Adam and Eve are summoned to judgment. But the first two acts are purely lyrical
and expository, and the last is masque-like in its
allegorical pageantry. This draft, therefore, has
only a nucleus of dramatic situation. The fourth
draft marks a development in two directions. In
the first place, it is more dramatic than its pre-
decessor in that the part of the Chorus is better
handled and the motives of the characters are more
explicitly stated. But the apparent improvement
may be due to the fact that this last outline
is longer than the others. The more interesting development is toward the epic form that
eventually was chosen. The story of Lucifer's
rebellion is introduced at the start, as in *Paradise
Lost*, and then narrated more fully later; the
outline suggests rather the episodic breadth of the
epic than the stricter unity of the drama; and
at the end a "masque of all the evils of this life
and the world" is called by the angel before
Adam's eyes, just as the messenger in the epic
brings the vision of the future before him. After
this vision, Adam submits and repents, as he does
in *Paradise Lost*. So, although this fuller draft
points toward a better dramatic treatment, it

more distinctly shows how Milton's deliberation was gradually leading him to the epic plan that was finally evolved.

But from these last two outlines the kind of drama that the poet contemplated is made obvious. He of course did not have in mind the English acting play. His tragedy was to be classical in structure, and, for the more easy presentation of matter lying beyond the natural scope of dramatic treatment, recital of incidents by an expositor or Chorus was to be freely resorted to. But the presence of allegorical characters in the outlines suggests the spirit of the Renaissance. Both drafts provide an ending resembling that of the popular court masque. In the fourth draft, especially, the masque of all the evils of life that passes before Adam resembles the pageantry of the court entertainment and the dumb shows of some Elizabethan plays. Milton's play, then, seems to hover between classical tragedy and Jacobean masque.

Yet the work under consideration was not suited either to tragedy or to masque. Its scope is too vast for actual drama, and its theme too lofty and too momentous in its consequences for the masque. The story involves two plots, the revolt of Lucifer and the fall of man, which are not only dissimilar in place and nature of action, but not synchronous, one, in fact, being the direct outcome of the other. This difficulty would not be insurmountable in a classical play, for the earlier action could be presented by narrative, as is done in *Oedipus Tyrannus*. But, in addition, the two plots involve the whole creation, Heaven, Earth, and Hell, and to relegate to an ever ready expositor all that happens in these spiritual realms would be open to serious objection. The characters of the play are equally unsuited to dramatic handling; for to dramatize them renders them too materialistic. The arming of Michael, for instance, in Vondel's *Lucifer* is simply the preparation of a Dutch soldier for battle, and carries the reader no whit beyond the soldier's common experience. And finally, the story of Adam's fall, as Milton interpreted it, is not tragic, for it ends with assured hope for Adam and his posterity. In all these respects the theme was ill-adapted for dramatic treatment, and Milton, abandoning his early plans, chose ultimately the more suitable epic form.

By so doing the poet obviated the difficulties that have been pointed out. He could carry the whole story, though not necessarily in strict chronological order, from its beginning in Lucifer's revolt in heaven, to its close, the expulsion of forgiven man from the Garden of Eden. The two great incidents of the "fable" could be placed in their strict sequential relationship, yet at the same time could be kept jointly before the reader. Unhampered by the limited possibilities of theatrical representation, the poet by allusion and the exercise of imagination suggests vividly and powerfully what lies beyond human vision. Hell's conclave, the adoration of the angels before God's throne, the sylvan splendors of Eden, lie within the scope of the poet. It is a story, also, which conforms to the critical theories of what the epic should be. In the epic, according to Tasso, the hero is not involved in action that rouses the on-looker's pity and fear; instead, he is the con-trolling agent in a story that brings out all the generosity and bravery of a truly noble character.[1] Milton does all this with an artist's skill. Just how he has given strict unity to so comprehensive a theme, observing at the same time many of the epic conventions, a following chapter will explain. There can be no question that Milton's final de-cision in favor of the epic as against tragedy was fortunately made.

Thus through long years Milton's plans for his great life's undertaking slowly but steadily took shape. And when the opportunity came, after the laying down of the Latin secretaryship, to return to his chosen studies, Milton was ready, in spite of blindness and thwarted hope, to carry it to completion. The epics of his mature years and his one drama naturally represent the best part of his life and thought. His scholarship, his ripened philosophy of life, his ideals undimmed by disap-pointment and misfortune, all go to make these poems what they are. It was almost inevitable that the poet should disregard the literary con-vention that bids the epic and dramatic poets

[1] *Dell' Arte Poetica*, pp. 34–35.

keep themselves apart from their work. Bernard
Shaw in recent years has flippantly defied this
convention for the dramatist; Milton seriously
and almost unconsciously defied it for the epic
poet. He speaks of himself in his blindness with
all the fervor of a lyric poet. He describes his
mode of composition and his conception of what
the modern epic should be. Homer, the other
blind epic poet, never obtrudes in this way; but
Milton, who wrote after a life of thought with a
conscious literary purpose, could not refrain. And
who would ask such concealment of him? He is
always at his best when his thoughts turn to self.
The finest passages in his prose are autobiographical, for he could speak of personal affairs
with dignity and of his ideals with conviction.
And this intrusion of the subjective brings into
his last poems a glimpse of the earnest life and
the high ideals that made possible the fulfilment of
his literary aspirations.

Chapter III

The True Bearing of Milton's Prose

THE attainment of Milton's high ambition, the growth of which has just been traced, was long delayed by more urgent duties of another sort. He was still in Italy, enriching his mind by study and converse with cultured literary men, when the disquieting news came of political troubles at home. At once the high-minded Puritan returned to London that he might hold himself in readiness should the call come. He had a few pupils to occupy him, and his own studies; but the muse in those days seemed indeed thankless, and the poet soon found himself embroiled in the work of pamphleteering for the Puritan cause. From 1641, when his first tract appeared, until 1660, when his last plea for liberty was penned, his energies were given mainly to the needs of the hour. Only the edition of the Minor Poems, published in 1645, and several of his finest sonnets, would remind the Puritan patriots, and perhaps even the author himself, that a rare, poetic genius was apparently being sacrificed in the cause of freedom.

There can be no doubt that Milton regarded
the enforced occupation of pamphleteering as a
serious interruption to his life's purpose. He
would have preferred studious retirement had it
not been for the realization that knowledge and
intellectual power bring grave responsibilities, to
which he, like the prophets of old, was forced
to sacrifice his ease and pleasure. He turned to
controversy unwillingly; "for surely," he declared,
"to every good and peaceable man, it must in
nature needs be a hateful thing to be the dis-
pleaser and molester of thousands; much better
would it like him doubtless to be the messenger
of gladness and contentment." [1] But his responsibilities had to be met; "when God commands to
take the trumpet, and blow a dolorous or a jar-
ring blast, it lies not in man's will what he shall
say, or what he shall conceal." So the Hebrew
prophets had shouldered their burdens, and Milton meant not to shirk his. "This I foresee,"
he reasoned with himself, "that should the church
be brought under heavy oppression, and God have
given me ability the while to reason against that
man that should be the author of so foul a deed;
or should she, by blessing from above on the industry and courage of faithful men, change this
her distracted estate into better days, without the
least furtherance or contribution of those few
talents, which God at that present had lent me;
I foresee what stories I should hear within my-

[1] *Ch. Gov.*, 2, pp. 474-476.

self, all my life after, of discourage and reproach."
It was this sense of duty — "the enforcement of
conscience only "— that induced him to abandon
poetry, and give his energies to controversy, in
which he had, as he remarked, the use but of his
left hand.

Other poets had already been forced to abandon their chosen work, and some, like Milton,
were metamorphosed into pamphleteers. William
Browne's cravings for the ideal had found expression in the first two books of *Britannia's Pastorals*,
published in 1613 and 1616. Then, before the
third part appeared some twenty years later, the
author's inspiration had largely waned, and finally
was altogether stamped out by the rapidly increasing civil discord. Browne, yielding to the
sterner temper of the day, next planned a serious
epic, but to no purpose. His most un-Miltonic
motto, "noli altum sapere," stamped on the bind-
ing of the Salisbury manuscript of his poems, suggests that he had neither the power nor the real
desire for such continued effort. In the same way,
George Wither first followed the diversions of the
courtly poet and later, abandoning the muse,
served the Puritan cause with both sword and
pen. Thus serious affairs of state interfered with
the work of the Caroline poets, just as public interests had checked the activity of the Tudor
poets before the time of Spenser. Few like Herrick and Sir Thomas Browne could remain un-
concerned, and Milton gave almost twenty years

of his life to active service of the cause he
championed.

It needs no further demonstration to show that
Milton was called from his chosen studies to this
other field of labor, and that he made the change
with real regret. It is more difficult, however, to
determine how much he was forced in consequence
to alter his ideals and to forsake his ultimate aim.
Possibly, in the work of these years his character
and power of thought took firmer shape. If that
be so, his prose will mark a steady, if not rapid or
even conscious, progress toward the three great
poems of his maturity.

Turning to Milton's prose with this consideration in mind, the reader is at once impressed by
the absence in the tracts of that high artistry that
is noticeable in all his poems. The sure sense of
form displayed in *L'Allegro* and *Il Penseroso* and
the firm structure of *Paradise Lost* are in the prose
works wholly lacking. Some, like the *Animadversions*, are thrown loosely together, chapter by
chapter, as Milton doggedly follows the argument
of his opponents. The best of his treatises, the
Areopagitica, shows a careful plan, but its coher-
ence is not plainly marked and its progress is not
even. *The Ready and Easy Way to Establish a
Free Commonwealth* is more simple and direct than
the bulk of his prose. But in general, the poet's
sense of form, which proved its surety in many
different types of poetry, lay in abeyance in prose
composition.

This want of careful structure is in part accounted for by the haste with which the author was forced to write and by his partial preoccupation with other duties. *The Tenure of Kings and Magistrates* was composed in the few weeks, possibly not more than three, preceding the execution of King Charles. The other tracts were hurried off as they were needed; yet Milton was by nature a conscious artist, who composed with extreme care. This alone would account for some of the formlessness of the tracts.

Yet they are really not formless compared with other prose writings of the time. Prose as an art developed later than poetry, and in the seventeenth century huge folios like Burton's *Anatomy of Melancholy* were inclusive in content rather than compact and orderly. Details of style might be considered, for euphuism had taught the possibilities of sentence structure. Sir Thomas Browne gave the greatest care to the revision of his *Religio Medici*, and Milton, if one may judge from his comments on Bishop Hall's brief sentences, evidently prided himself on his long and sonorous, though often unparsable, periods. His diction, too, is strong and picturesque. But the paragraph, which Milton developed so artistically in his epics, is left in his prose a huge, misshapen thing. The rhetoric of the seventeenth century did not demand a symmetrical and steadily progressive development of thought in prose. A useful art had not learned, except

in rare cases like Sir Thomas Browne's, to be
also fine.

In this respect Milton's prose differs from his
highly artistic poetry; but in more essential respects there is true similarity between them. It
could hardly be otherwise, since Milton engaged
in prose composition with the same high motives
that moved him as a poet. He was not seeking
praise or official position, and could truthfully
say that he had made himself "never even a
shilling the richer by those exertions." His one aim
was "that the truth, which had been defended
by arms, should also be defended by reason." He
may have drilled at one time with the trained
bands of London; but he never enlisted in the
Puritan army, for there were hundreds of robust
men, he thought, able to defend the truth in arms,
to the few capable of supporting it by sound argument, which, he adds, "is the best and only
legitimate means of defending it."[1] This being
his motive, Milton is never altogether engrossed
in the ephemeral phases of the controversies he
engaged in. He rises above them and leads the
reader on to the realm of great ideas and universal
principles where as a poet he loved to dwell. In
these higher moods, and they are frequent, there
is little to distinguish Milton, the pamphleteer,
from Milton, the poet.

Milton early became interested in the promotion
of liberty, which he regarded as the one doorway

[1] *Sec. Def.*, I, pp. 219, 238, 243.

to truth. For this single reason he abandoned his first intention of entering the church, in whose service he saw no chance of personal freedom, and devoted his energies to the new cause. His own words best explain his motives.[1]

I saw that a way was opening for the establishment of real liberty; that the foundation was laying for the deliverance of man from the yoke of slavery and superstition; that the principles of religion, which were the first objects of our care, would exert a salutary influence on the manners and constitution of the republic; and as I had from my youth studied the distinctions between religious and civil rights, I perceived that if I ever wished to be of use, I ought at least not to be wanting to my country, to the church, and to so many of my fellow-Christians, in a crisis of so much danger; I therefore determined to relinquish the other pursuits in which I was engaged, and to transfer the whole force of my talents and my industry to this one important object.

To this general statement Milton adds a full list of his controversial writings in behalf of liberty, and then closes the account of this chapter in his life with the characteristic summary: "Such were the fruits of my private studies, which I gratuitously presented to the church and to the state; and for which I was recompensed by nothing but impunity; though the actions themselves procured me peace of conscience, and the approbation of the good; while I exercised that freedom of discussion which I loved."

[1] *Sec. Def.*, I, pp. 257–261.

The long-continued service of liberty that is here described might have been rendered impersonally, for there is an objective mode of defending even heart-felt truth. But Milton was never given to self-effacement. In his great epic he thrice speaks frankly of his own condition, and once again, as he describes Abdiel, the angel of truth, his thought is colored with consciousness of self.[1] Curiously, he seems to have had greater reticence in speaking of himself in his prose; "for although a poet," he explains, "soaring in the high reason of his fancies, with his garland and singing robes about him, might, without apology, speak more of himself than I mean to do; yet for me sitting here below in the cool element of prose, a mortal thing among many readers of no empyreal conceit, to venture and divulge unusual things of myself, I shall petition to the gentler sort, it may not be envy to me."[2] Nevertheless, he speaks much of himself in his prose. In the *Second Defence* he outlines briefly the course of his life; in *An Apology for Smectymnuus* he discusses with dignity his character and ideals. Here one sees the "love of God" and the "pious and just honoring of ourselves," which Milton regarded as the two principles "of all godly and virtuous activities in men." The powerful and unique personality of the author pervades all his prose. Many readers have been inclined to cen-

---

[1] *P. L.*, 3, ll. 1–55; 7, ll. 1–39; 9, ll. 13–47.
[2] *Ch. Gov.*, 2, p. 477.

sure Milton for such apparent egotism, but there was justification for it. His opponents had misrepresented certain facts in his life and had traduced his character. To-day, such untrue aspersions are easily refuted and offset by the general diffusion of knowledge through the medium of the press. But in the seventeenth century there was no such ready means of appeal, and the slandered controversialist had to meet his opponent on the field where he found him stationed. Milton might believe that "the best apology against false accusers is silence and sufferance, and honest deeds set against dishonest words";[1] nevertheless, self-respect would urge some reply, and for that his own tracts offered the best medium.

Moreover, Milton was tempted for another reason to speak of self. All his prose treatises bore some direct relation to personal affairs. He composed his plea for the freedom of the press after he had been summoned before the Lords for violation of the Licensing Act. The *Tractate on Education* was the outgrowth of his actual experience in teaching. The discussions on divorce were prompted by his domestic troubles, and several of his ecclesiastical tracts were written to aid Thomas Young and other friends. It was easy, therefore, for Milton to obtrude into his argument, especially since his conduct in life could scarcely be dissociated from the principles he held. He mentions himself, however, with unfailing

[1] *Animadversions*, 3, p. 97.

truth and dignity, and his prose would lose much of its warmth and human interest if these passages were stricken out.

Some of Milton's controversial works do not rise above the immediate occasion that brought them forth. For example, the *Animadversions upon the Remonstrant's Defence against Smectymnuus* is as unlovely a piece of argument as its crabbed title might indicate; it is contentious, bitter, petty, and nothing more. Other works, fortunately, rise far above the mere point at issue. If the analogy would not be taken too rigidly, it might be said that these disputatious arguments compare with Milton's great prose as the *Epitaphium Damonis* compares with *Lycidas*. The elegy in memory of Diodati is equal to its occasion, whereas *Lycidas* is greater than its occasion. So it is with the most vital of Milton's controversial works; the civil or domestic troubles that prompted them are forgotten as the author rises to great principles and enduring truths. Freedom of thought and speech, confidence in the power of truth and righteousness, the observance of God's will — these are the great principles for which Milton contends.

Such disparity between his best and worst work is one of the most striking features of Milton's prose. He may descend at times, and indeed often, to the trivialities and abusiveness of seventeenth-century disputation; but like the bird at sea he soars again to the higher elements of reason

and truth where was his home. He can argue on
the burning of the Ephesian books by St. Paul's
converts as though it actually were a matter of
moment, but immediately he rises above such
petty contention to the sublime truth: "He that
can apprehend and consider vice with all her baits
and seeming pleasures, and yet abstain, and yet
distinguish, and yet prefer that which is truly
better, he is the true warfaring Christian." No
flight could be more sudden from triviality to truth.

An extensive and varied collection of such en-
nobling, universal truths might easily be made
from these prose treatises. "Honest liberty is the
greatest foe to dishonest licence." "He who would
not be frustrate of his hope to write well hereafter
in laudable things, ought himself to be a true
poem." "It is not the common law, nor the civil,
but piety and justice that are our foundresses."
"It is not so wretched to be blind, as it is not to
be capable of enduring blindness." "To be still
searching what we know not, by what we know,
still closing up truth to truth as we find it, . . .
this is the golden rule in theology, as well as in
arithmetic, and makes up the best harmony in a
church." These are only a few sentences taken
half at random from passages that do not happen
to be quoted elsewhere.

Sentences like these, which stud the pages like
jewels, render these pamphlets truly Miltonic.
The author's mind, however, reveals its power and
elevation not simply in such fragments; many

great questions are handled at length with sustained power. Milton's long plea for the freedom of the press has been accepted as the true gospel of intellectual liberty. His analysis of the relation between church and state, in which he showed himself far in advance of his age, is clear and incisive throughout.[1] His exposition of the only true function of government is so thoroughly sound that it should be quoted:

To govern well is to train up a nation in true wisdom and virtue, and that which springs from thence, magnanimity (take heed of that), and that which is our beginning, regeneration, and happiest end, likeness to God, which in one word we call godliness. . . . This is the masterpiece of a modern politician, how to qualify and mould the sufferance and subjection of the people to the length of that foot that is to tread upon their necks. . . . To be plainer, sir, how to solder, how to stop a leak, how to keep up the floating carcase of a crazy and diseased monarchy or state, betwixt wind and water, swimming still upon her own dead lees, that now is the deep design of a politician. Alas, sir! a commonwealth ought to be but as one huge Christian personage, one mighty growth and stature of an honest man, as big and compact in virtue as in body; for look what the grounds and causes are of single happiness to one man, the same ye shall find them to a whole state, as Aristotle, both in his Ethics and Politics, from the principles of reason, lays down.

Milton, one is too often reminded, was an idealist and not a practical reformer; but this force-

[1] *Reform.*, 2, pp. 392 ff., 409 ff.; *Ch. Gov.*, 2, pp. 487 ff.

ful passage displays a clear insight into sound
principles of statecraft.

In formulating this theory of the functions of
church and state, Milton did not allow himself to
be blinded by the glamor of a name; what Bacon
had called the idols of the market-place never deceived him. Hence he follows liberty as a sound
principle, not a fetish. "None can love freedom
heartily but good men," he asserts. Such freedom, of course, depends not on a mere form of
government, but on the physical and moral health
of the nation; it is "the fruit of piety, of justice,
of temperance, and unadulterated virtue." Hence
he insists, "Unless you will subjugate the propensity to avarice, to ambition, and sensuality,
and expel all luxury from yourselves and from
your families, you will find that you have cherished a more stubborn and intractable despot at
home, than you ever encountered in the field."[1]
Such was Milton's conception of true liberty, a
freedom which depends on mind and character,
and which requires of those who would enjoy it
"a complete and generous education, that which
fits a man to perform justly, skilfully, and magnanimously all the offices, both private and public,
of peace and war."

This whole ideal of liberty is permeated with
the philosophy of individualism. A nation pros-
pers only when its citizens are sound, since the
commonwealth is but "one huge Christian per-

[1] *Sec. Def.*, 1, p. 295.

sonage." External restraints and coercion, therefore, can bring no vital improvement, and any
real reform must operate through the inner lives
of the individuals of the nation. Consequently,
instead of trying to force people to do right, teach
them to choose it. "A dram of well-doing," Milton argues, "should be preferred before many
times as much the forcible hinderance of evil-
doing"; we must learn "to ordain wisely as in
this world of evil." Such freedom may result
for a time in wrong. But in the end man can
learn to "apprehend and consider vice with all
her baits and seeming pleasures, and yet abstain, and yet distinguish," and so become "the
true warfaring Christian." [1] The establishment
throughout the world of such individual self-
restraint — the love of that which is really good,
Milton calls it — was the object of all Milton's
philosophy.

It is hard to determine the exact limits of Milton's liberal philosophy. In several of his early
tracts he seems to deny the state any power of
coercion over the individual; in his last writings
he apparently assumes the position of a reactionary. The inconsistency is not so great as it
appears. Even in his earliest republican tracts
his argument that the king is subject to the will
of the people must be taken to apply to the better
elements of the populace and not what we to-day
call the "masses." And although he argues at

[1] *Areopagitica*, pp. 75, 68.

the same time that Christians should have liberty
to elect their own ministers and formulate their
own doctrine, he adds the qualification, provided
their capacity, faith, and prudent demeanor com-
mend them. He never believed that atheists
should be tolerated, for their teaching was sub-
versive of all social life; nor papists, for they were
dangerous politically to the English state. This
is the general purport of his early teaching, and
he did not change these views radically in his
latest tracts, where he seems to advocate not a
democracy but an oligarchy, composed of the
wisest and most godly citizens of the country.

The most reactionary of Milton's publications
is *The Ready and Easy Way to Establish a Free
Commonwealth.* Written when the overthrow of
the commonwealth and the restoration of the
Stuart monarchy were imminent, this treatise is
primarily designed as a warning. But the student's interest is most aroused by the exposition
it gives of the "ideal commonwealth." Such a
state must be ruled by a single representative assembly, whose members should be chosen from
the best and ablest of the citizens. They are to
be selected not by a strictly popular vote, and are
to hold office for life or until incapacitated or con-
victed of misdemeanor; for frequent general elec-
tions bring instability and corruption into the
state. In addition to this national assembly,
whose character is far from being democratic,
there are to be local assemblies, which are to

legislate on purely local affairs, and in which men receive training for service in the national council. But the right of suffrage is to belong only to "such people as are rightly qualified," and the members of the grand council must be aristocrats because they, better than common men, can be counted on for honest and efficient service. In its general trend the argument seems to be that the common people should not have the opportunity of choosing what is unsafe; the rule of the wise minority is preferable to the license of the majority.

The Ready and Easy Way certainly seems to repudiate much that Milton had more boldly defended in earlier years. Impending dangers had forced him to sacrifice something to safety. In a letter of this same period he wrote: "Whether the civil government be an annual democracy or a perpetual aristocracy, is not to me a consideration for the extremities wherein we are, and the hazard of our safety from our common enemy." It was no time, he felt, to theorize on liberty in the abstract when the first essentials of actual liberty, gained after so hard a struggle, were threatened. Experience, too, had taught him a practical lesson; for the lawlessness and dissensions that disgraced the Puritan parliament naturally forced on all thinking men a distrust of democracy. In 1660 the Puritans seemed unable to rule wisely, and the people were bent on the re-establishment of the old monarchy. But

the restoration of the Stuarts, Milton was con-
vinced, would result in a renewal of the old
tyranny in aggravated form. Why, then, grant
the people the whim of the moment, which is
bound to be regretted too late; why allow ill-
advised liberty to destroy the last vestiges of true
freedom? "More just it is," Milton concludes
"that a less number compel a greater to retain,
which can be no wrong to them, their liberty,
than that a greater number, for the pleasure of
their baseness, compel a less most injuriously to
be their fellow-slaves."

Is it unfair to conclude that Milton had been
forced only temporarily to abandon the more sublime ideal of liberty and tolerance that he had
proclaimed in the *Areopagitica?* The three great
poems that he wrote after his retirement from
active life reaffirm the earlier views. *Paradise
Lost* traces the progress of the individual to that
perfect conformity with the divine will which
alone is freedom. The liberty to do right is again
upheld in *Paradise Regained* and *Samson Agonistes.*
This same confidence in the power of righteousness
underlies the *Areopagitica*, where Milton asserts:
"And though all the winds of doctrine were let
loose to play upon the earth, so truth be in the
field, we do injuriously by licensing and prohibit-
ing to misdoubt her strength. Let her and falsehood grapple; who ever knew truth put to the
worse, in a free and open encounter?" In one
way or another *Comus*, the two epics, *Samson*

Agonistes, and the author's best prose support this bold declaration; it was the settled conviction on which his life's work rested.

So confident is Milton of the eventual triumph of his ideals that he writes often with the vigor and the fervor of a prophet. His prose more truly than De Quincey's can be called "impassioned"; for Milton's is inspired by principle where De Quincey's is moved by sentiment more than normal or healthy in its acuteness. It is provoking sometimes to see Milton take his eye from his subject to soar aloft into the realm of the ideal. Nevertheless, no other style of thought would be characteristic of him; his loftiness of purpose and intensity of conviction must find vivid expression in what he calls the "hymn in prose."

One such hymn in the *Areopagitica* is widely known: "Methinks I see in my mind a noble and puissant nation rousing herself like a strong man after sleep, and shaking her invincible locks; methinks I see her as an eagle mewing her mighty youth, and kindling her undazzled eyes at the full midday beam; purging and unscaling her long-abused sight at the fountain itself of heavenly radiance; while the whole noise of timorous and flocking birds, with those also that love the twilight, flutter about, amazed at what she means, and in their envious gabble would prognosticate a year of sects and schisms." Very similar is the style of the closing pages of *Reformation in England*, where historical review yields place to fervent

prayer and prophecy. In such prose Milton's most
unique powers are seen. He can harass an opponent mercilessly, hammering away with vividly
concrete diction and vigorous sentences; he can
state facts in clear, compact form, as he does in
The Ready and Easy Way; he can handle deftly
the ordinary weapons of seventeenth-century
controversy. But he is most himself when the
substance of his treatise brings him face to face
with some great principle. Then the power of his
intellect, the intensity of his convictions, and
the artist's mastery of expression work in perfect
unison, and the prose controversialist becomes the
poet.

There are in all many dreary wastes of controversy in Milton's prose that will be remembered
only by the historian. And even he can learn of
Bishop Hall, the Primate of Armagh, or the
unfortunate Salmasius better elsewhere than from
the pages of Milton. But there is also a great
deal in the prose works that the world could ill
afford to lose. Great thought, high principle,
courageous adherence to ideals, elevate most of
his tracts above the disputes of the day, and
bring them into kinship with his poetry.

The keynote or master passion of all Milton's
prose was love of liberty. Liberty, however, did
not signify to Milton the power to do one's own
pleasure. "There is not that thing in the world,"
he asserts, "of more grave and urgent importance
throughout the whole life of man, than is dis-

cipline." [1]   Hence true liberty did not seem incompatible with honest servitude; Abdiel replies to Satan:

> Unjustly thou deprav'st it with the name
> Of servitude, to serve whom God ordains,
> Or Nature.

In accordance with the same principle it follows "that none can love freedom heartily but good men." [2]   Liberty, therefore, is the willingness and ability to do what should be done.   That such freedom depends on character has already been shown, but one more quotation may reinforce this truth.   In the *Second Defence* Milton insists that "real and substantial liberty" is rather to be sought from within than from without, and that its existence depends, "not so much on the terror of the sword, as on sobriety of conduct and integrity of life." [3]   Laws and political institutions may repress freedom, but they never can create it; for true freedom is within us, a possession of our own souls.

This interdependence of freedom and virtue furnishes the text for those eloquent closing pages of the *Second Defence*.   The fervent appeal to Cromwell; the grateful recognition awarded Fleetwood and the other Parliamentarians; and all of that general appeal to the English public beginning, "For it is of no little consequence, O citizens, by what principles you are governed, either in acquiring liberty, or in retaining it when acquired.   And

---

[1] *Ch. Gov.*, 2, p. 441.   [2] *Tenure*, 2, p. 1.   [3] *Sec. Def.*, 1, p. 258.

unless that liberty which is of such a kind as arms can neither procure nor take away, which alone is the fruit of piety, of justice, of temperance, and unadulterated virtue, shall have taken deep root in your minds and hearts, there will not long be wanting one who will snatch from you by treachery what you have acquired by arms," — these passages are among the most eloquent that Milton ever penned.

But liberty and individual rectitude, valued in this noble spirit and brought into perfect unison, are, after all, simply the high means to a still more sublime end. Personal character, according to Milton's philosophy, insured liberty for the individual and the state; and freedom and character together lead to the highest goal, truth. This is the ultimate end of all human endeavor — the attainment again of that divine truth lost by Adam. Listen once more to Milton's own eloquent words in *Areopagitica:*

Truth indeed came once into the world with her divine Master, and was a perfect shape most glorious to look on; but when He ascended, and his apostles after him were laid asleep, then straight arose a wicked race of deceivers, who, as that story goes of the Egyptian Typhon with his conspirators, how they dealt with the good Osiris, took the virgin Truth, hewed her lovely form into a thousand pieces, and scattered them to the four winds. From that time ever since, the sad friends of Truth, such as durst appear, imitating the careful search that Isis made for the mangled body

of Osiris, went up and down gathering up limb by limb
still as they could find them. We have not yet found
them all, lords and commons, nor ever shall do, till her
Master's second coming; He shall bring together every
joint and member, and shall mould them into an immortal feature of loveliness and perfection. Suffer not
these licensing prohibitions to stand at every place of
opportunity forbidding and disturbing them that continue seeking, that continue to do our obsequies to the
torn body of our martyred saint.

With the most unconquerable idealism Milton
firmly believed that truth would once again prevail on earth. Even in the darkness of his last
years, he still had sublime confidence in her immortal strength. He would have reaffirmed then
the words of *Areopagitica*:

For who knows not that truth is strong, next to the
Almighty; she needs no policies, nor stratagems, nor
licensings to make her victorious; those are the shifts
and the defences that error uses against her power:
give her but room, and do not bind her when she sleeps,
for then she speaks not true, as the old Proteus did,
who spake oracles only when he was caught and bound,
but then rather she turns herself into all shapes except
her own, and perhaps tunes her voice according to the
time, as Micaiah did before Ahab, until she be adjured
into her own likeness.

It was for the furtherance of truth through the
upbuilding of character and the safeguarding of
liberty that Milton strove in his controversial
works. They may be marred by the bitterness

of party strife, but the final impression that they leave with the reader is of a high-minded idealist working in prose for those same master passions that control his verse — liberty, temperance, virtue, and truth.

Chapter IV

Epic Structure of *Paradise Lost*

ALTHOUGH Milton was widely read in literature and well versed in critical theory, he composed no systematic treatise on epic poetry, as others had done. In his prose he several times describes the mission of the inspired poet — the abstinence he must practice; the integrity of character that should be his, since no man can be "truly eloquent who is not withal a good man" and whose life is not itself "a true poem"; and the loftiness of the ideal to which he must hold. The epics of Homer, Virgil, and Tasso, the tragedies of Sophocles and Euripides, and the poetry of *Job*, *Revelation*, and the *Song of Solomon*, are highly praised by him; for such poetry brings uplift to the character of a people. "These abilities," Milton sees, "wheresoever they be found, are the inspired gift of God, rarely bestowed," and the function of poetry is "to imbreed and cherish in a great people the seeds of virtue and public civility, to allay the perturbations of the mind, and set the affections in right tune; to celebrate in glorious and lofty hymns the throne and equipage of God's almightiness, and what he works, and what he suffers to be wrought with high providence in his church; to sing victorious agonies of martyrs and saints, the deeds and triumphs of just and pious nations, doing valiantly through faith against the enemies of Christ; to deplore the general relapses of kingdoms and states from justice and God's true worship." [1] If poetry achieves all this, "the paths of honesty and good life . . . will then appear to all men both easy and pleasant, though they were rugged and difficult indeed." Thus Milton described the high calling of a poet. But he nowhere gave an accurate and inclusive definition of epic poetry or formulated rules, as Tasso and others had done, for the guidance of those who would attempt its composition.[2]

The reason that Milton wrote no more specifically on the nature of heroic poetry may be that he thought much more of content than of form. He calls *Job*, for example, an epic simply because its theme is so truly heroic. But a student can gather for himself Milton's theory of the epic from a careful study of *Paradise Lost* and *Paradise Regained*. They were the work of years and were written with classical poetry as a model and with Renaissance critiques as guides. Yet in his epics Milton followed no models slavishly, for he realized that form is determined not by rule or

[1] *Ch. Gov.*, 2, p. 479.
[2] His most precise definition, found at the close of the *Second Defence*, simply restates Aristotle's doctrine.

precedent but by the thought to be expressed. Hence he adapted the pattern of the epic to his own ends, and wrote as a creative artist. It will be possible to show how thought and form in his epics perfectly harmonize.

Paradise Lost opens with the usual epic invocation. But neither here nor elsewhere does Milton adopt a literary convention that is unfitting. Where Homer calls only on the goddess and where Virgil invokes the muse alone, Milton seeks aid of two higher powers. The first is the Heavenly Muse, called in a later book Urania, of whom he asks the same inspiration that had enkindled the ancient Hebrew poets; the other is the Holy Spirit, who alone can reveal hidden mystery. Each represents "eternal wisdom," but the latter, in higher degree. It is both a prophet's vision and an artist's hand that the poet craves, that he may rise to the "height of this great argument" and "justify the ways of God to man."

After this invocation, Milton, still following the accepted pattern of the epic, expounds the theme of *Paradise Lost*. Homer outlines his story in the opening lines of the *Iliad:* "Sing, goddess, the wrath of Achilles, Peleus' son, the ruinous wrath that brought on the Achaians woes innumerable, and hurled down into Hades many strong souls of heroes, and gave their bodies to be a prey to dogs and all winged fowls; and so the counsel of Zeus wrought out its accomplishment from the day when first strife parted Atreides, king of men, and noble

Achilles." Virgil, in the same way, forecasts the contents of the *Aeneid:* "Arms I sing, and the man, who first from the shores of Troy came, Fate-exiled, to Italy and her Lavinian strand — much buffeted he on flood and field by constraint of Heaven and fell Juno's unslumbering ire; much suffering in war, withal, ere he could found him a city and bring his gods to Latium; — author of the Latin race, and the sires of Alba, and the walls of Lofty Rome." So Milton here asks the question:

> Say first — for Heaven hides nothing from thy view,
> Nor the deep tract of Hell — say first what cause
> Moved our grand Parents, in that happy state,
> Favoured of Heaven so highly, to fall off
> From their Creator, and transgress his will
> For one restraint, lords of the World besides.
> Who first seduced them to that foul revolt?

The answer that follows states clearly the cause of Lucifer's revolt and its connection with the sin of Adam. Thus Milton presents together the two episodes, or plots, of which the epic is composed, and shows their sequential relationship. An epic convention again becomes a means to an end; it enables him to outline firmly, as no other mode of treating this much-used subject does, the two stories, and to show their causal relationship. The theme, in brief, is the downfall of Lucifer and the sin and punishment of man.

This brief outline, furthermore, enables Milton to disregard, without sacrifice of clearness, the chronological order of events, and to begin, after

epic fashion, *in medias res*. The great epic antagonist is at once introduced lying with Beelzebub
in the pit of Hell. The scene is first suggestively
described:

> A dungeon horrible, on all sides round,
> As one great furnace flamed; yet from those flames
> No light; but rather darkness visible
> Served only to discover sights of woe,
> Regions of sorrow, doleful shades, where peace
> And rest can never dwell, hope never comes
> That comes to all, but torture without end
> Still urges, and a fiery deluge, fed
> With ever-burning sulphur unconsumed.

The imagination can dwell almost indefinitely on
such a phrase as, "no light, but rather darkness
visible." In the same suggestive manner Satan,
lying amid such torture undaunted and defiant,
is described in words that carry far beyond their
actual reach into the realm of the imagination.
Then more precise description follows, with an
amplitude of figure and allusion characteristic of
Milton's epic style. First the picture is completed
of that

> Seat of desolation, void of light,
> Save what the glimmering of these livid flames
> Casts pale and dreadful.

Then Satan is depicted:

> With head uplift above the wave, and eyes
> That sparkling blazed; his other parts besides
> Prone on the flood, extended long and large,
> Lay floating many a rood, in bulk as huge
> As whom the fables name of monstrous size.

The comparisons that follow to mythical giants
and the leviathan of Norwegian seas preserve in

this more definite picture the vagueness that stimulates the imagination so strongly in the first. Satan's personality and the setting are made as vivid as any dramatic scene or character could be, yet they embrace more. The rallying of the fallen soldiery at their leader's call, the council of war in Hell, and the self-delegated mission of Satan into the surging elements of Chaos, afford material of epic scope. Nevertheless, although the whole scene is too stupendous, and the characters too superhuman, for the drama, each of the great leaders possesses dramatic individuality. Milton has selected a powerful moment for his epic beginning, when half his story has been already enacted and when the other half is still to be carried through.

How much of epic and dramatic force Milton obtains by beginning thus *in medias res* is revealed by a comparison of *Paradise Lost* with the Old English poem on the same subject attributed to Caedmon. His arrangement of details is not strictly chronological; for his full account of the revolt of Lucifer is preceded by the story of the creation. Nor can one fail to see in this Biblical paraphrase an artistry in proportions and a simple dignity and power in phrase. By telling early of the creation of man, and by leading directly and rapidly to the temptation in the garden, Caedmon, if he it were, focusses attention on the main theme, the fall. The poem, however, lacks the passages of highest power, the artistic variation from scene to scene, and the rising and falling of poetic feeling, that distinguish *Paradise Lost;* the light and shade of Milton's art were altogether beyond the old Saxon poet. One was a chronicler of real power, the other, a creative master.

In another respect, also, these first two books of *Paradise Lost* display the author's sense of form. By so beginning *in medias res,* he is able to keep before the reader from the beginning the two episodes of which the epic is composed. No other poet has succeeded so perfectly in connecting the rebellion of Lucifer with the fall of man. Vondel, for example, simply appends in the fifth act of *Lucifer* the later story. And indeed, since the stories are not coincident in time, and since each presupposes its own locale, it would be hard to tell how the dramatist could make them one. But from the beginning of the epic the two are joined. The first lines direct attention to the disobedience of Adam and explain the reason for Lucifer's treachery; the council of war terminates with Satan's determination to effect man's ruin, and his departure to find the newly created earth. Thus the two stories are woven indissolubly together, and a real artistic unity is made possible.

The action of *Paradise Lost,* which begins here in the depths of hell, moves on through Chaos to heaven itself and earth. Each separate scene is filled with the spirit of the unknowable, for even the Garden of Eden transcends all earthly scenes in its beauty and peace; and Milton's pictures are necessarily suggestive rather than precise. Nevertheless, the locale of the poem must be made clear, and the relative position of the separate parts of creation have to be plainly fixed. Satan, as the poem states, fell for nine days through space, a distance thrice the radius of the earth. Between the heaven which he lost and the hell where his prison-house was to be, intervened the hitherto untraversed Chaos, where unstable elements of hot and cold, moist and dry, still surged and tossed without control. Just beneath the bounds of this heaven hung the universe we know, or the ten spheres, which, according to the Ptolemaic system of astronomy, revolve about our earth as center. On all sides of the fixed realm of heaven lay the Empyrean; all about the universe and hell was Chaos. Of the three realms hell is most specifically described. In the center lay a lake of fire, fed by four streams, Cocytus, Styx, Phlegethon, and Acheron. This was surrounded by a parched desert where the council of war was held, and this, in turn, was bounded by the river Lethe and a frozen continent, "beat with perpetual storms of whirlwind and dire hail." At some spot on the edge of this frozen zone, stood the gate of hell, and through it Satan passed on his hazardous journey into Chaos. He finally alighted on the outermost of the ten concentric spheres, the Primum Mobile, whence he gained his first glimpse of this earth, the object of his search, far below. After his departure from hell, Sin and Death built a bridge between that realm and earth, and the universe, as Milton depicts it, was complete.[1]

It takes more than a superficial reading to make of the isolated statements regarding the relative position of these places a clearly defined picture. In each particular case the precise detail of fact is colored by poetic imagery and allusion till it leaves with the reader a sense of limitless reach. The description of Chaos, for example, is made up of an abundance of detail; but the darkness, the murky clouds, and the swirl of the elements remove the picture from the world of space and time far into the illimitable, unknown universe.

That Milton should conceive his vast epic background in accordance with the teachings of the Ptolemaic astronomy has aroused much comment. Over a century before the composition of the poem, Copernicus had proclaimed the new teaching, and by the middle of the seventeenth century his theory must have been everywhere known, if not generally accepted, among scholars.[2] Why then did Milton, who had studied mathematics and science in his youth at Horton, and whose sympathy for Galileo was twice expressed, hold to the old belief? Evidence is not wanting in *Paradise Lost* that he accepted, or at least understood, the Copernican system. Adam, it is true,

[1] Two somewhat different diagrams of this universe can be found in Masson's and Himes's editions of the poem. The above statement is based chiefly on Himes's arrangement.

[2] Consult T. N. Orchard: *The Astronomy of "Paradise Lost."*

supposes the earth to be the center about which all the stars and planets move, and his error is not unnatural. Satan, too, in a speech which upholds the most unworthy view of life, approves the same opinion.[1] But Raphael, whose vision is more than mortal, reveals the truth:

> What if the Sun
> Be centre to the World, and other Stars,
> By his attractive virtue and their own
> Incited, dance about him various rounds?
> Their wandering course, now high, now low, then hid,
> Progressive, retrograde, or standing still,
> In six thou seest; and what if, seventh to these,
> The planet Earth, so steadfast though she seem,
> Insensibly three different motions move?
> Which else to several spheres thou must ascribe,
> Moved contrary with thwart obliquities,
> Or save the Sun his labour, and that swift
> Nocturnal and diurnal rhomb supposed,
> Invisible else above all stars, the wheel
> Of Day and Night; which needs not thy belief,
> If Earth, industrious of herself, fetch Day,
> Travelling east, and with her part averse
> From the Sun's beam meet Night, her other part
> Still luminous by his ray. . . .
> But whether thus these things, or whether not —
> Whether the Sun, predominant in heaven,
> Rise on the Earth, or Earth rise on the Sun;
> He from the east his flaming road begin,
> Or she from west her silent course advance
> With inoffensive pace that spinning sleeps
> On her soft axle, while she paces even,
> And bears thee soft with the smooth air along —
> Solicit not thy thoughts with matters hid:
> Leave them to God above.

[1] See *P. L.*, 8, ll. 5–38; 9, ll. 99–109; 8, ll. 122–168.

These astronomical truths are conveyed by the angel in the form of a question, and one can only infer that Milton was ready to accept them. Since the angel is God's messenger, he doubtless expounds the facts as Milton understood them, and he leaves the question unsettled only because Adam, or man in general, has more important lessons to learn than these. Thus Milton censured, as Ruskin did, a too boundless intellectual curiosity, and would have man fix his attention on his prime concern — his relation to God.[1]

Besides feeling that man can realize his position in the world and his relations to God as well under the Ptolemaic as the Copernican system of thought, Milton may have found the wealth of association gathered about the old belief poetically more inspiring than the cold fact still being adduced in support of the new. Poets have often clothed their deepest convictions in the language of fancy. The great rose of heaven was to Dante a symbol, not a fact, and Milton himself beautifully harmonizes in *Lycidas* the legends of ancient mythology and the fundamental truths of Christianity. A belief, then, is surely permissible that Milton still retains what he knows to be an erroneous conception of the universe, simply for its greater emotional appeal, though at the same time he states the facts, and with approval, that science was already teaching.

But it was not essential for Milton early in the

[1] *P. L.*, **7**, ll. 118–130. Ruskin, *Eagle's Nest*, Lecture 4.

course of the poem to expound all these astronomical principles; for the function of the first
two books in the scheme of the poem as a whole
is to present vividly certain scenes and characters powerful enough to serve as foundation for a
long epic narrative. The third book, in like manner, lays the theological and philosophical groundwork of *Paradise Lost*. Milton's purpose is to
"justify the ways of God to man," or, in other
words, to explain the relationship between good
and evil. But only God can expound the vexing
problem of the origin of evil in a sinless universe.
And so God, in this council about his throne, explains why he, in creating the angels and man,
left them free to choose either the right or the
wrong.

> I made him just and right,
> Sufficient to have stood, though free to fall.
> Such I created all the Ethereal Powers
> And Spirits, both them who stood and them who failed;
> Freely they stood who stood, and fell who fell.
> Not free, what proof could they have given sincere
> Of true allegiance, constant faith, or love,
> Where only what they needs must do appeared,
> Not what they would?   What praise could they receive,
> What pleasure I, from such obedience paid?

Thus God justifies the endowment of angels and
man with the freedom of the will; he has next to
predict and justify the consequences of that freedom. Man, he foresees, will sin and punishment
must be inflicted if justice is to prevail. Of this,
man can not complain, for God's foreknowledge in
no wise constrained him to sin. Endowed with

a sense of right, and fortified by ample warning
regarding the nature and consequences of sin,
man has only himself to blame if he is forced to
suffer. Justice is God's first motive. Unfortunately, many readers have failed to see in Milton's
system of thought a second ruling motive, love.
This principle, which is hinted at in the fourth
and fifth lines of the poem, is here emphatically
proclaimed. God explains that while Satan, who
fell "self-tempted, self-depraved," can claim no
forgiveness, man may expect grace. The plan of
atonement that Christ proposes is at once accepted, and man's eternal salvation is assured.
Love here triumphs over justice, as it does also
in Dante's *Divine Comedy*, and God's ways toward
man are summed up in his own words:

> In mercy and justice both,
> Through Heaven and Earth, so shall my glory excel;
> But mercy, first and last, shall brightest shine.

This long discourse on dogma has been severely
censured as lying without the realm of poetry.
Unquestionably, the discussion of such matters
purely for theological reasons, would be out of
keeping with the end of true art. But Milton
sees that, if he is to justify, by concrete example,
the ways of God to man, he must make these
points clear. Adam must be made to feel both
the justice and the love of God, and the principles that lie at the bottom of that justification
must be established. Hence the third book, after
the epic and dramatic incidents that have pre-

ceded it, lays the foundation for the philosophy that the poem would teach.

Although the main purpose of the third book is philosophical, it does not fail to strengthen, also, the structure of the poem as a whole. In the first place, God's explanation brings together the two plots, Satan's revolt and man's fall, and introduces a hero for the first. Satan for all his might can not be the hero of the epic; yet not till Christ offers himself as a sacrifice does the reader see what mightier force is to conquer. In the second place, the philosophical explanation of the triumph of good over evil prepares the way for the concrete handling of the same truths in later books. In these respects, then, the third book is vitally a part of the whole poem and on artistic grounds is justified.

After this theological exposition the poet returns to his narrative. Under Uriel's direction Satan finally reaches the earth and enters Eden. The locus of the poem here suddenly changes from the spiritual to the visible universe; but the change is not especially noticeable. The Earthly Paradise is still, before the sin, almost a part of heaven; an angel watch guards it, angels pass and repass between it and heaven, and a glory of verdure and a splendor of light make it a place divine. Milton uses for his picture details of landscape that he has seen or read of. A glimpse or two of flowery English meadow land or pasture, rich suggestions of Oriental herbage, amplified and colored by a comparison of Eden with three gardens famous in classical literature and a fourth known in Abyssinian history, leave the impression of Paradise and not of earth. The objects that we know have been transformed by the alchemy of poetry to a sublimated form; it is as though we were among the Platonic archtypes of things.

The most important contribution, however, of the fourth book to the epic is not this change of place from the unseen to the seen universe; it is the development of Satan's character. What of heroic might he seemed to possess during the scenes in hell he loses here. Among his fallen lieutenants his aspect possessed force and even grandeur of a certain sort;

> Round he throws his baleful eyes,
> That witnessed huge affliction and dismay,
> Mixed with obdurate pride and steadfast hate.

But in the serener peace of Eden and the pure light of heaven, Satan's debasement is obvious to all, and to no one more than to him;

> Now conscience wakes despair
> That slumbered; wakes the bitter memory
> Of what he was, what is, and what must be
> Worse; of worse deeds worse sufferings must ensue!

Nothing remains for him but courageous, though hopeless, defiance of God. Even the adoration of his followers brings only heightened misery; and he describes his actual state in the words:

Which way I fly is Hell; myself am Hell;
And, in the lowest deep, a lower deep
Still threatening to devour me opens wide,
To which the Hell I suffer seems a Heaven.

Realizing this, Satan consecrates himself to evil doing:

All good to me is lost;
Evil, be thou my Good.

And, as he speaks, his face is disfigured by ire, envy, and despair. To the old-time pride that first prompted revolt, and to the rage against the angelic victors, is now added a third, and the most poignant, torment, hatred of man whom he finds in bliss. From this point on, Satan loses all even of the falsely heroic that he once possessed.

After these incidents, Raphael is dispatched by God from heaven to convey to Adam full warning of the presence of his arch enemy and the certain coming of temptation. The flight of the angel through the heavens gives opportunity for splendid epic description, and the meeting of god with man is in accordance with epic convention; but the chief value of this incident is its ethical significance. A portion of the story is trivial; for meal-time in *Paradise Lost* is not the most inspiring moment, and the angel's scientific exposition of the nutrition of planets is fancy and not fact. But the poem's aim is to justify God's dealings with man, and man must be duly warned of coming danger if he is to be held justly accountable for his fault. Hence the angel fully explains the situation, and, after stressing the necessity for obedience, narrates the story of Satan's defeat, without failing at the close to point again the moral. The book closes with this warning:

> Thus, measuring things in Heaven by things on Earth,
> At thy request, and that thou may'st beware
> By what is past, to thee I have revealed
> What might have else to human race been hid —
> The discord which befell, and war in Heaven
> Among the Angelic Powers, and the deep fall
> Of those too high aspiring who rebelled
> With Satan: he who envies now thy state,
> Who now is plotting how he may seduce
> Thee also from obedience, that, with him
> Bereaved of happiness, thou may'st partake
> His punishment, eternal misery;
> Which would be all his solace and revenge,
> As a despite done against the Most High,
> Thee once to gain companion of his woe.
> But listen not to his temptations; warn
> Thy weaker; let it profit thee to have heard,
> By terrible example, the reward
> Of disobedience. Firm they might have stood,
> Yet fell. Remember, and fear to transgress.

But the account of the war in heaven, which has often been ridiculed, is in other respects closely related to the structure of the epic as a whole. Such narration of past events, of course, is a part of the established epic convention. Aeneas reviews for Dido the story of the Trojan War, just as the angel here tells of the conflict in heaven. The angel's story, also, exhibits Satan still in his glory, as he was before the transformations in hell and on earth, second only to

God in glory and might. And finally, here again the two plots are firmly joined. Satan first revolts, withdrawing with him to his "quarters in the North" the "third part of Heaven's host," because of jealous hatred of the newly created Son. The revolt and the ensuing punishment are directly antecedent to the creation of man and the temptation, since man was created to replace the fallen angels, and since Satan's desire to ruin Adam was prompted by thirst for revenge. All this is brought before the reader during Raphael's narrative. Satan, the great epic antagonist, in all his might; Christ, the hero of the first plot; and Adam, the hero of the second and the representative of the whole race, are brought together in the story. Thus these incidents are made indispensable to the development of the epic, both as a story and as a philosophy of life.

The combat in heaven, moreover, furnishes the most strictly epic portion of the narrative. The movements of the two armies, the prowess of Abdiel and Michael in single combat against Satan, and the speeches of the warriors are reminiscent of Homer. But Milton wishes the reader to see something more than the epic qualities of the narrative. The angel, as he ends his story, reminds Adam that, in describing the great battle between good and evil, he has used language comprehensible to man. In other words, the details of the combat are not literally true, but simply express the truth symbolically, in terms of human experience. Here Milton, it may be, forgets consistency, for Adam in Paradise would know nothing of armor or of cannon; but the central truth of the story is obvious. It is, in the first place, a warning, which renders Adam liable to punishment in case he sins. And, in the second place, it symbolizes the whole relation of good to evil, which is the theme of the epic. Abdiel clearly personifies truth, for God thus judges his service:

> Well hast thou fought
> The better fight, who single hast maintained
> Against revolted multitudes the cause
> Of truth, in word mightier than they in arms,
> And for the testimony of truth hast borne
> Universal reproach, far worse to bear
> Than violence; for this was all thy care —
> To stand approved in sight of God, though worlds
> Judged thee perverse.

And Abdiel defines Christian liberty as Milton himself would do:

> Unjustly thou deprav'st it with the name
> Of servitude, to serve whom God ordains,
> Or Nature: God and Nature bid the same,
> When he who rules is worthiest, and excels
> Them whom he governs.

The battle itself brings "rout deformed" and "disorder foul," which connote disorder in the spiritual life; and the final defeat of Satan signifies plainly the triumph of right over wrong. Moreover, the struggle of evil in heaven exactly resembles the same struggle on earth, and man must overcome evil, as God did, if order and justice are to rule. This is the meaning of the story.

From the overthrow of Satan, the great climax of one plot, to the creation of man, the first incident in the second, an easy transition is made. Adam, after listening to Raphael's relation, questions him further:

> But, since thou hast voutsafed
> Gently, for our instruction, to impart
> Things above Earthly thought, which yet concerned
> Our knowing, as to highest Wisdom seemed,
> Deign to descend now lower, and relate
> What may no less perhaps avail us known —
> How first began this Heaven which we behold
> Distant so high, with moving fires adorned
> Innumerable; and this which yields or fills
> All space, the ambient Air, wide interfused,
> Embracing round this florid Earth; what cause
> Moved the Creator, in his holy rest
> Through all eternity, so late to build
> In Chaos; and, the work begun, how soon
> Absolved.

In this manner the two stories are brought together. They really belong side by side; for, although one is the consequence of the other, they express the same moral truth. Furthermore, their close juxtaposition is not without its purely artistic value, since it brings variation of mood and diversity of description into the poem. In these two central books of the epic, then, the seventh and the eighth, the second phase of Milton's theme is definitely presented.

In the next incident of the poem, the temptation and fall, Satan meets his earthly enemy, man, as he had formerly met Christ in Heaven's war.

The same conflict is now waged on earth, with different weapons and with apparently different results; for the good seems here to fall before the evil. Adam, who in Eden upholds the cause that Abdiel, Michael, and Christ upheld in heaven, is too weak to resist the subtler attack now made by Satan, and yields. It may seem, therefore, that Adam's position is not analogous to Christ's; but the outcome is such that Adam foresees at least an eventual victory. Man with Christ's aid can emerge victorious on earth, as Christ and his angels prevailed in heaven.

The story of the first conflict between these two opposing forces was told in the language of classical poetry; the second story follows the then accepted Biblical tradition. Yet the temptation is not easily suited to poetic treatment; for the upright movements of the serpent and his glibness of speech are in themselves ludicrous either for epic or drama. In Milton's early drafts for a tragedy on the subject, no hint is given of the serpent's actual *rôle*. Vondel slights the whole incident in narrative, and Caedmon, disregarding Biblical tradition, allows Satan to assume the guise of a messenger from God. Milton, too, might have simplified the problem; for in *Paradise Lost* Satan enters the Garden enwrapped in the mists of the underground river, and could appear to Eve as a disembodied spirit. But Milton does not seek to avoid the incongruity of the old Hebrew story; instead, he allows Satan to explain why he selected that particular disguise, and then adds as brilliant a picture of the serpent as Keats paints in *Lamia*.

Milton by still further amplification enhances the effectiveness of the story of the temptation. In this regard, it is interesting to compare his version with Caedmon's. Caedmon, in the first place, brings the tempter to his victim in the form of an angel-messenger.[1] He goes in that guise to Adam himself, not to Eve, and, representing himself to be one of God's messengers come from heaven with a divine commission, orders Adam to eat of the fruit of the tree, that he may add to his wisdom and power and so honor his creator the more. Adam, however, sees through Satan's deceit and repels him. Then the impostor approaches Eve and urges her to obey God's command, that her husband may be pardoned for his disobedience. Eve, completely deceived, obeys the supposed injunction, thinking thereby to save her husband from punishment. At once she fancies that the fruit has given the promised knowledge, and she is then able to persuade Adam that he too should obey God's will. Completely deceived, he yields. Milton's version of the story is quite different. His beginning, it must be admitted, is inferior to Caedmon's; for a talking serpent as tempter is far less probable than an angelic messenger. And Milton's tempter proceeds along different lines from Caedmon's. Going first to Eve,

[1] See 2 *Cor.*, 11. 15.

he begins by flattering the woman for her beauty
and by arousing her curiosity to know how the
power of speech became his. But this is not enough
to lead her to eat, when she is told that his human powers have come from the fruit of the forbidden tree. Hence Satan changes his tactics and
shows her how good and not evil must follow the
eating of the apple. God, he explains, laid the
injunction simply out of jealousy, and only in a
mystical sense — the putting off a lower for a
higher nature — could death be said to result from
the eating. Persuaded by this more subtle argument, and also impelled, it is to be regretted, by
the hunger of noon-time, Eve eats the apple.
Then, wishing that Adam may enjoy the blessing
she fancies is hers, she goes to him and urges him
to eat. He at once perceives the evil she has done
and reproaches her. But because he does not wish
to be separated from her, or to enjoy more of
divine favor than she, he tries to persuade himself that God's injunction has been nullified by
the serpent's eating of the fruit, and finally, in
part persuaded by these specious arguments and
in part overcome by Eve's physical charms, he,
too, eats and Satan's end has been gained.

Caedmon's version of the temptation is more
simple and credible than Milton's; but Milton's
is stronger and better suited to his purpose. Caedmon minimizes the fault of the guilty pair by assigning them the most creditable motives possible.
Eve sins through pure unselfishness and obedience,

and Adam sins through misunderstanding; both have been deceived. Milton gives them baser motives. In Eve, selfishness and envy as well as vanity are the ruling motives; in Adam, uxoriousness and self-deception. These baser motives are more fitting for the theme; for Adam's sin is intended to embrace all sin, and Satan, if he has power to inspire any feelings, would inspire the most sordid. Because of the baseness of Adam's motives, furthermore, the punishment that follows is rendered more just, and the regaining of paradise in the end, a more signal instance of divine mercy.

Moreover, the significance of the sin is more effectively set forth by Milton than by Caedmon. Satan, on achieving his victory in the medieval poem, laughs like a Mephistopheles, whereas Satan in *Paradise Lost* slinks off in shame and terror. The most dire consequences attend the sin. While Adam ate the fruit,

> Nature gave a second groan;
> Sky loured, and, muttering thunder, some sad drops
> Wept at completing of the mortal Sin
> Original.

Further changes are wrought in nature by divine command, when the guilty pair go forth to earn their subsistence by hard toil. Although this, like so many other incidents in the poem, is derived from classical literature, Milton's thoughts seem to be less on the Golden Age than on Biblical story and the general moral law that good and

evil have power to alter environment for better or
for worse. In that symbolical light most of the
transformations that follow the sin are to be taken.
A bridge is built by Sin and Death to link earth
with hell — a detail that needs no elucidation.
Satan, on his return, announces victory to the
fallen angels, but instead of shouts of triumph
hears "a dismal, universal hiss," and feels himself transformed to serpent form, doomed to eternal
degradation. Milton amplifies the detail, be sure,
not only as fact, but as a symbol of the trans-
forming, imbruting power of sin on the soul. Such
debasement is even more noticeable in Adam and
Eve. Love at once is turned to lust, and, after
lust has been satiated, shame, recrimination, and
pangs of conscience come to destroy the peace of
Eden. Milton makes the scene of carnal passion
between Adam and Eve as repulsive as possible,
because he wishes to contrast it with Adam's first
meeting with Eve, where all was love and holi-
ness. By the degrading power of sin all that once
was good has been turned to evil.

But the epic was not designed by Milton for
such an end as this. Adam has sinned, punishment must follow, and earth no longer can be a
paradise. But the suggestion of a happier destiny for man was given at the beginning in the
words: Till one greater Man
        Restore us, and regain the blissful seat,
and the plan of atonement was devised and accepted in the council scene of the third book. Christ,

the victor over Satan in one plot, becomes the ally and savior of the defeated hero in the second plot. Adam, thus strengthened by the spirit of the heavenly victor, through long years of probation and schooling learns to conquer the mighty power of evil. The long recital of Hebrew history that fills most of the last two books of *Paradise Lost* simply shows how this conquest is to be gained. It shows what God's ways to man really are; it exhibits the dire consequences of evil-doing; and it formulates the great principles of right-living. Christ then appears in the Garden as intercessor and judge, to fulfill the promise early recorded, and Satan and man receive their diverse sentences together. The stories of the two conflicts are thus for the last time brought together; Christ and Adam, who have fought the hero's fight against the great antagonist, stand united. Two stories have been told, widely different in outward character, and extensive in scope, so that they afford ample and widely varied material for a long epic. But all this wealth of material has been directed by the poet to a single end. The two stories are first connected by the closest sequential relationship. They are also really parallel, being simply different expressions of the same great principle, the warfare of good against evil. Both lead to the same end — a paradise lost and regained; and here at the conclusion they stand once more united in closest unity. The epic, therefore, is an artistic whole.

In this chapter the structure of *Paradise Lost* has been discussed, in the attempt to show what the epic form for this narrative material should be. The poem has its deeper meaning, which has been hinted at here, but which will be more fully presented in a later chapter. For the exposition of this same deep thought other poets have used other forms of literature. Shakespeare presented it dramatically on the stage. Later authors have expounded it in psychological novels and in analytical poems. But Milton's chosen form was the epic, and what this involved in his mind the discussion just concluded has been designed to show.

Chapter V

The Sources of *Paradise Lost*

(a) *The Bible*

MICHAEL'S forecast of the future in the closing books of *Paradise Lost* recalls to the well-read man several other such prophetic visions. He·may think first of the revelation given by Anchises to Aeneas of the heroes, yet unborn, who were to found and rule the Roman state. He may remember, also, the very similar, though more discursive, historical resumé found in Sylvester's translation from Du Bartas, the *Diuine Weekes and Workes*, which Milton read in boyhood. And even more forcefully the analogy may suggest itself with the divine revelation given to Daniel, the first portion of which, as in *Paradise Lost* and indeed also in the *Aeneid*, is given in vision, and the last portion in narrative. If this one division of the poem so gives indication of Milton's classical scholarship, his knowledge of the *Bible*, and his acquaintance with English literature, it is but typical in this respect of the poem as a whole. *Paradise Lost* is a literary epic, and behind it, giving detail, color, and artistic form,

are the literatures of various peoples of widely
different times. Israel and ancient Greece and
Rome, Italy of the Renaissance, Elizabethan England, and possibly Holland of the seventeenth
century, contributed to *Paradise Lost* at least some
part of their best thought and their highest sense
of the poetic art.

Many old-time readers of *Paradise Lost*, conversant mainly with Biblical literature, were accustomed to read the epic solely as a sacred poem.
It was the favorite reading, for example, of John
Bright. Such minds found in it, vividly retold, a
large portion of *Old Testament* history, all focussed
about two or three incidents of human experience
on which rests the Christian faith. Milton's version came to be regarded almost as canonical Scripture, and his story of the expulsion of Lucifer, the
creation of man, and the temptation and fall in
the Garden of Eden, has become part of the web
and woof of English thought. The burning pit of
hell, the state of innocence and bliss in Eden, the
eating of the apple, and even minor details like
Adam's naming of the birds and animals, are presented as authentic facts. Although Milton's
narrative is more full and varied than Biblical history, his spirit accords with that of the Hebrew
chroniclers, and his own confidence in divine inspiration is more than once expressed. Almost
unconsciously, therefore, the Bible-reading Christian has ascribed to Milton the divine guidance
which he prayed for of the

> Celestial Patroness, who deigns
> Her nightly visitation unimplored,
> And dictates to me slumbering, or inspires
> Easy my unpremeditated verse.

It is wrong, however, whether one accepts *Genesis* as history or myth, to interpret *Paradise Lost* simply as recital of fact. Its theme, as the following chapter will attempt to show, is far deeper and more enduring than that, and there is evidence in the poem that Milton wished us to read the story not so much for the facts as for the truths expressed. In *Christian Doctrine*, to be sure, he displayed his unquestioning trust in the literal reading of the Scriptures. He had formulated his own system of belief, as he insisted every one should do, by a close study of the *Bible;* no verse, however insignificant, was purposely disregarded or perverted by false interpretation. So Milton justified even the anthropomorphic representation of Deity, on the ground that God must have revealed himself to man in the form in which he wished himself to be conceived. But Milton realized that "both in the literal and figurative descriptions of God, he is exhibited not as he really is, but in such a manner as may be within the scope of our comprehensions." Milton, therefore, did not assert "that God is in fashion like unto man in all his parts and members." He simply believed that "as far as we are concerned to know, he is of that form which he attributes to himself"; for God certainly employed language in his revelation adequate to teach the great truths that man should know. And these truths, rather than a literal statement of the revelation, are of vital concern to the human race.

In *Paradise Lost* Milton shows himself even more willing to recognize this distinction between a literal and a symbolical revelation of the divine. Dante explains in his letter to Can Grande four different ways of interpreting Biblical stories; Milton, I think, would justify two. He found in the *Bible* an historical record which he accepted as true not in all respects to actual facts but to God's ultimate purpose. On that ultimate purpose our attention is focussed in *Paradise Lost*. Had Milton regarded the epic as matter of fact history, he could not have incorporated, without serious inconsistency, so much legendary material from ecclesiastical and even pagan sources; for in matters of faith "we are expressly forbidden to pay any regard to human traditions." In his poem he follows Scriptural story, because it seems the fittest way of describing the eternal conflict between good and evil; but he adds also non-Biblical details that are in keeping with it. He specifies, for example, the apple as the forbidden fruit; he adopts a pagan cosmography; and he founds his war in heaven on Homeric traditions. Like portions of the sacred story itself, these details seemed fit symbols of the truths that the *Bible* aims to teach.[1]

[1] See *Ch. Doctr.*, chaps. 30, 2.

This distinction between facts and the enduring
truths revealed by them is plainly brought out in
Paradise Lost.[1] Raphael is careful in the poem to
explain to Adam:

> And what surmounts the reach
> Of human sense I shall delineate so,
> By likening spiritual to corporal forms,
> As may express them best — though what if Earth
> Be but the shadow of Heaven, and things therein
> Each to other like more than on Earth is thought.

A similar reminder is given later that spiritual
truth must sometimes be expressed in materialistic form. Milton believed that some foundation
of fact in the heavenly kingdom lay behind this
symbolical revelation. But since God has with-
held the exact nature of those facts, there must be
something deeper than fact for man to learn from
Bible story. Ever the poet's thought is centered on
the truth itself and not on its expression. It was
the sin of Adam and not its trivial form, the
eternal consequences of evil and not the flames of
hell, that were truths to him. The poem does
not read the facts of creation literally. *Paradise
Lost* follows the Biblical narration of the work of
the six days, as Du Bartas and all others had
done, but plainly sanctions a less literal interpretation of the story. This is the meaning of the
lines:

> Immediate are the acts of God, more swift
> Than time or motion, but to human ears
> Cannot without process of speech be told,
> So told as earthly notion can receive.

[1] *P. L.*, 5, ll. 571–576; 6, ll. 893–896; 7, ll. 176–179.

Thus the poet interpreted the Scriptures liberally
and philosophically, and *Paradise Lost* depends
less upon a literal acceptance of ancient myths
than upon the moral significance of what those
myths denote.

Milton was not the first to teach that the language of the Scriptures is accommodated to the
finite character and experience of the human mind.
John Colet, the founder of St. Paul's School, where
Milton himself received his early education, expounded in exactly this way the first chapters of
Genesis.[1] In one of his letters to Radulphus, Colet
explains that Moses in the account of creation,
"Setting aside matters purely Divine and out of
the range of the common apprehension, proceeds
to instruct the unlearned people, by touching
rapidly and lightly on the order of those things
with which their eyes were very palpably conversant, that he might teach them what men are,
and for what purpose they were born, in order that
he might be able with less difficulty to lead them
on afterwards to a more civilized life and to the
worship of God — *which was his main object in
writing*." Hence Moses assigns to separate days
the creation of different parts of the universe,
which were in actuality created simultaneously
before the beginning of time. And hence he mentions in the story of creation those objects that
man most often sees, in what would seem to man
a natural order. For Moses wished to speak of

[1] Seebohm, *The Oxford Reformers*, pp. 25–36.

heavenly things in a manner not derogatory to God, yet in words that could be easily comprehended by the unlettered men whom he addressed. The lines just quoted from *Paradise Lost* exactly express Colet's theory of "accommodation."

Because Milton read the *Bible* in the spirit of a poet and philosopher, he drew his inspiration mainly from the poetic books of the *Old Testament* and the *Apocalypse* and *Jude*, rather than from the uncolored narrative of the Pentateuch. The exegesis of early churchmen, too, and general Biblical tradition enter in to give body and amplitude to the episodes that constitute the foundations of the epic. The temptation in the Garden is told in *Genesis*, but nothing is given there of Lucifer's fall, and it is from scattered references in the Prophets and the *New Testament* that Milton gathers his material. The creation is outlined in *Genesis*, but Milton was inspired more by the glowing songs on the creation in *Job* and the *Psalms*. The reader seldom stops to consider from how many Biblical and extra-Biblical sources Milton's story is drawn. Hence Lamartine, like many others, looked upon *Paradise Lost* as "the dream of a Puritan fallen asleep over the first pages of his Bible." [1] Although the idea is not inexplicable, it is altogether erroneous.

For even the bare outlines of the story of Lucifer's fall, Milton had to look to the later books

[1] Quoted from Himes, *Paradise Lost*, p. x.

of the *Bible*, since the writings of the Pre-exilic
period say nothing of Satan or demonology. God,
to the early Hebrews, was the sole ruling spirit,
and all acts, good and bad alike, were attributed
to him. Even the Satan of *Job* was a spirit allowed by God to tempt the man of Uz. In the
later Biblical writings, however, a system of
thought derived from the dualistic philosophy of
the Persians and Babylonians appears, and God is
represented as ever opposed and threatened by
his arch-foe, the spirit of evil. In *Zechariah* and
First Chronicles, however, the evil spirit is still not
independent of God.[1] This dualism is carried
further in the *New Testament*, where Christ is
represented as openly at war with Satan.[2] Luke
writes, "And he said unto them, I beheld Satan
as lightning fall from heaven." St. Peter speaks
still more explicitly: "God spared not the angels
that sinned, but cast them down to hell, and delivered them into chains of darkness, to be re-
served unto judgment." Jude makes essentially
the same statement, and the author of the Apocalypse carries on the tradition in the verse: "And
the great dragon was cast out, that old serpent,
called the Devil, and Satan, which deceiveth the
whole world: he was cast out into the earth, and
his angels were cast out with him."[3] Like the
theologians of his time, Milton, of course, was

---

[1] *Zech.*, 3. 2; *1 Chron.*, 21. 1 ff.
[2] *Matt.*, 4. 1; 13. 39; *John*, 14. 30.
[3] *Luke*, 10. 18; *2 Peter*, 2. 4; *Jude*, 1. 6, 7; *Rev.*, 12. 7–9; 20. 1–3.

inclined to understand the serpent mentioned in *Genesis* as Satan; but his epic embodies these dualistic ideas that the Hebrews learned during their exile.

The reader can therefore understand why Michael is the first angel commissioned by God in *Paradise Lost* to lead the fight, and why he is chosen to meet Satan in single combat. The picture simply amplifies the verse in *Revelation:* "And there was war in heaven: Michael and his angels fought against the dragon: and the dragon fought and his angels." [1] About this verse and several others the tradition of centuries has gathered a vast wealth of legend.

In exactly the same way a few passages in the *Bible*, extended and colored by uncanonical writings, have given Milton his conception of the angelic hosts. In the canonical scriptures only two angels are mentioned by name — Michael, called "the chief of princes," and Gabriel. Two others, Raphael and Uriel, are named in the Apocrypha, and in *Zechariah* and *Revelation* the seven angels are alluded to who "run to and fro through the whole earth." [2] These, too, are mentioned by Milton. The complete idea of the heavenly hierarchy, which was elaborated by Dionysius, the Areopagite, did not directly influence Milton; for although in *Paradise Lost* he

---

[1] See *Rev.*, 12. 7; *Jude*, 1. 9; *Daniel*, 8. 16; 9. 21.

[2] *Tob.*, 12. 15; 2 *Es.*, 5. 20; *Zech.*, 4. 10; *Rev.*, 5. 6. See *P. L.*, 3, l. 650.

speaks often of the heavenly hosts, "each in his hierarchy, the Orders bright," he alludes only once to the nine definite orders.[1]   He employs the names "dominions," "thrones," and "powers" vaguely, as they are used in the *Bible*.   He seems to have been influenced, therefore, only in a general way by ecclesiastical tradition, and his pictures of the angels in heaven and their movements through the universe, are simply a poet's rendering of hints found in the *Bible*.

To illustrate this point a single passage will suffice:

> Him all his train
> Followed in bright procession, to behold
> Creation, and the wonders of his might.
> Then stayed the fervid wheels, and in his hand
> He took the golden compasses, prepared
> In God's eternal store, to circumscribe
> This Universe, and all created things.
> One foot he centred, and the other turned
> Round through the vast profundity obscure,
> And said, "Thus far extend, thus far thy bounds;
> This be thy just circumference, O World!" [2]

This is a poet's glowing vision of the verse in *Proverbs:* "When he prepared the heavens, I was there: when he set a compass upon the face of the depth."   Two other richly poetic hymns on the creation moved the poet profoundly.   The Lord's reply from the whirlwind to convince Job of man's insignificance among the wonders of creation, and the Psalmist's song of praise and grati-

[1] *P. L.*, 1, l. 737; 5, ll. 748–750.
[2] *P. L.*, 7, ll. 221–231; *Prov.*, 8. 27–29; *Job*, 38; *Ps.*, 104.

tude were ever before him. Each clause of these two chapters is in essence a poem, and one can trace them in expanded form in the epic. "Man goeth forth unto his work, and to his labour, until the evening," for example, finds place in the fifth and ninth books of *Paradise Lost*, where Adam's joyous labor in the Garden is portrayed. The whole psalm breathes, if anything, a vivid sense of God's unfailing presence on earth. The Psalmist did not conceive of him as dwelling, since the work of creation, apart from man in heaven; his thought is that God still moves in every part of his handiwork. Milton, too, has this same conviction of the ever-present, in-breathing spirit of God throughout his creation. In other words, Milton holds the poet's conception of creation, not the annalist's or theologian's.

On almost every page of the epic, this same quickening spirit of the *Bible* has left its impression. It does not reveal itself mainly in open allusions to Biblical incidents or characters. The number of the fallen angels may be suggested by the comparison:

> As when the potent rod
> Of Amram's son, in Egypt's evil day,
> Waved round the coast, up-called a pitchy cloud
> Of locusts, warping on the eastern wind,
> That o'er the realm of impious Pharaoh hung
> Like Night, and darkened all the land of Nile.

Similarly, the stairway from heaven to earth is likened to the ladder of Jacob:

> The stairs were such as whereon Jacob saw
> Angels ascending and descending, bands
> Of guardians bright, when he from Esau fled
> To Padan-Aram.[1]

Such definite comparisons give the epic a concreteness and a Biblical coloring that it needs. But they are less numerous, I think, than exactly similar allusions to classical history and legend, and reveal the influence of the Scriptures in possibly the least vital aspect.

Of more importance to the poem are the numerous expansions of Biblical statements or thoughts. Some of those relating to the creation have already been noted, and they are really too numerous to list. Two passages of the Gospel of John underlie the expanded figure:

> As when a prowling wolf,
> Whom hunger drives to seek new haunt for prey,
> Watching where shepherds pen their flocks at eve,
> In hurdled cotes amid 'the field secure,
> Leaps o'er the fence with ease into the fold;
> Or as a thief, bent to unhoard the cash
> Of some rich burgher, whose substantial doors,
> Cross-barred, and bolted fast, fear no assault,
> In at the window climbs, or o'er the tiles.[2]

The passage contains reminiscences also of Homer and Virgil, reminding us again that *Paradise Lost* is a composite, literary epic; but the foundations of the description are the verses: "He that entereth not by the door into the sheepfold, but climbeth up some other way, the same is a thief and a rob-

---

[1] *P. L.*, 1, ll. 338–343; 3, ll. 510–513.
[2] *John*, 10. 1–2, 12–14. *P. L.*, 4, ll. 183–191.

ber.   But he that entereth in by the door is the
shepherd of the sheep. . . . But he that is an hire-
ling, and not the shepherd, whose own the sheep
are not, seeth the wolf coming, and leaveth the
sheep, and fleeth; and the wolf catcheth them,
and scattereth the sheep."

In a similar way, Adam's brief lament over his
lost power and glory resembles Job's self-re-
proaches.[1]   Here is found compression rather than
expansion of the original.   And to the *Bible* Milton
seems to have turned instinctively as his thought
rose into "the Heaven of Heavens."   For this
representation of God he could find nothing adequate in the classics; he apparently failed to
remember Dante's radiant vision.   He turned, instead, to one of the Prophets, who exerted such
influence on both his prose and verse.   Ezekiel
approaches the Almighty in the vision of the
whirlwind, the four living creatures and the chariot,
the voice heard from the firmament above their
heads, and the sapphire throne.   Dante transposes
this wonderful vision to the *Purgatory*, and Milton, to describe Christ's going forth to battle,
renders it thus:

> Forth rushed with whirlwind sound
> The chariot of Paternal Deity,
> Flashing thick flames, wheel within wheel; undrawn,
> Itself instinct with spirit, but convoyed
> By four cherubic Shapes.   Four faces each
> Had wondrous; as with stars, their bodies all
> And wings were set with eyes; with eyes the wheels

[1] See Himes, *Paradise Lost*, p. 449.

> Of beryl, and careering fires between;
> Over their heads a crystal firmament,
> Whereon a sapphire throne, inlaid with pure
> Amber and colours of the showery arch.
> He, in celestial panoply all armed
> Of radiant Urim, work divinely wrought,
> Ascended; at his right hand Victory
> Sat eagle-winged; beside him hung his bow,
> And quiver, with three-bolted thunder stored;
> And from about him fierce effusion rolled
> Of smoke and bickering flame and sparkles dire.
> Attended with ten thousand thousand Saints,
> He onward came; far off his coming shone;
> And twenty thousand (I their number heard)
> Chariots of God, half on each hand, were seen.
> He on the wings of Cherub rode sublime
> On the crystalline sky, in sapphire throned —
> Illustrious far and wide, but by his own
> First seen.

Here, then, in one of the finest visions of the poem, where the great hero hurls his foe to "bottomless perdition," the poet is content to see the divine form through the eyes of the prophet.

In some cases it is a whole verse that finds its way into the poem. God in the council scene is seated on his throne, and

> On his right
> The radiant image of his glory sat,
> His only Son.

These lines reproduce the verse in *Hebrews:* "Who being the brightness of his glory, and the express image of his person, and upholding all things by the word of his power, when he had by himself purged our sins, sat down on the right hand of the

Majesty on high."¹   Again, Abraham remonstrates
in behalf of Sodom, "That be far from thee to do
after this manner, to slay the righteous with the
wicked"; and in a very similar situation Christ
says: That be from thee far,
            That far be from thee, Father, who art judge
            Of all things made, and judgest only right!

Even more interesting is the scrupulous fidelity
to the *Bible* of the lines,

            Because thou hast hearkened to the voice of thy wife,
and,
            In the sweat of thy face shalt thou eat bread.

More frequently, it is but a single word or phrase
that so brings to mind the language and the incidents of the Scriptures.   The words, "That he
may know how frail his fallen condition is," rest
on the verse, "That I may know how frail I am." ²
In the same way one may place together: "Thou
hast appointed his bounds that he cannot pass"
and "her [Babylon's] bars are broken," and

                    Whom no bounds
            Prescribed, no bars of Hell, nor all the chains
            Heaped on him there.³

Such passages must have come into the poem from
conscious reminiscences of the *Bible*.

    Much more frequent, of course, are the instances
of a word or words used by Milton, probably unconsciously, in a common Biblical sense.   "Both

¹ *Heb.*, 1. 3.   *P. L.*, 3, ll. 62–64.
² *Gen.*, 18. 25;   *P. L.*, 3, ll. 153–155.   *Ps.*, 39. 4;   *P. L.*, 3, l. 180.
³ *P. L.*, 3, ll. 81–83;   *Job*, 14. 5;   *Jer.*, 51. 30.

heaven and earth shall high *extoll* thy praises";
"*reaping* immortal fruits of joy and love"; "for
ever with *corruption* there to dwell"; "*renew* his
lapsed powers"; "soften *stony hearts*"; "*dead
in sins*"; "let thine *anger fall*"; "the *Powers of
Darkness* bound"; "all *knees* to thee *shall bow*," —
these are only a few of the countless examples that
might be adduced of Milton's unconscious borrowing of Scriptural phraseology.[1] Its presence is
most noticeable in strictly Biblical portions of the
poem, like this council scene in heaven or the
angel's revelation of the future to Adam; but all
parts are colored by the language of the Scriptures.

It is but natural that this should be true of a
poem so entirely Christian in intent. Although
Milton's aim is more than simple recital of Biblical
narrative, his whole poem, intended as it was to
justify God's ways with man, rests on Biblical
foundations. Incidents are taken from Hebrew
history, characters are borrowed and presented in
the traditional way, details of description are
copied, and the thought of the sacred writers is
reproduced. The workings of God's law, in short,
are given in the words of the inspired book.
Hundreds of such instances of relationship are
too obvious to need attention. Others are not so
conspicuous. Several times the poet's mind seems
fixed on the verse, "Mercy and Truth are met
together," from the Eighty-fifth Psalm, which he
had already translated. His whole report of the

[1] *P. L.*, 3, ll. 146, 67, 249, 175, 189, 233, 237, 256, 321.

heavenly council, with its argument against predestination and its explanation of the atonement,
follows the Scripture, as Milton understood it.
From a passage of *Philippians* he derives the
thought:

> Nor shalt thou, by descending to assume
> Man's nature, lessen or degrade thine own.
> Because thou hast, though throned in highest bliss
> Equal to God, and equally enjoying
> God-like fruition, quitted all to save
> A world from utter loss, and hast been found
> By merit more than birthright Son of God.[1]

Like Carlyle and Ruskin, Milton was so thoroughly imbued with the language of the *Bible*
that he used it unconsciously in all he wrote.

To study this aspect of *Paradise Lost*, comparison with Milton's *Christian Doctrine* is constantly
necessary. This prose treatise serves for the reader
as an intermediary between the *Bible* and the
poem, as perhaps it served also for the poet. As
proof of God's grace, *Christian Doctrine* cites the
verse, "And I will put enmity between thee and
the woman, and between thy seed and her seed;
it shall bruise thy head, and thou shalt bruise
his heel." This same thought, very similarly expressed, appears several times in *Paradise Lost*.[2]
One interested in such citations from the Scriptures may compare the ninth chapter of *Christian Doctrine* with various passages in the poem.
That the angels fell of their own accord; that the

[1] *P. L.*, 3, ll. 303–309. *Phil.*, 2. 6–10. See Himes, p. 315.
[2] *Gen.*, 3. 15. *P. L.*, 10, ll. 181, 191, 1031; 12, ll. 149, 233.

good angels are upheld by their own strength; that angels, and especially the seven of whom Uriel is chief, are sent to minister to all unbelievers; that Michael is chief of all angels; that the knowledge of devils is great, "but such as tends rather to aggravate than diminish their misery" — these are only a few of the thoughts in *Paradise Lost* for which full Biblical justification is given in *Christian Doctrine*.

In this scriptural epic the doctrines of seventeenth-century divines naturally find a place. Milton's motives in writing were not theological; for he was intellectually too independent to accept the dogma of any church, and his main purpose was philosophical and literary. He had studied the works of the Fathers and had been accustomed to read the most significant parts of their writings to his pupils; but he recognized no authority as final, and ever insisted that each man must formulate for himself, from divinely revealed truth, his own system of belief. He was thoroughly Protestant in his assertion that the Scriptures were given "for the use of the church of all ages," and that they were so written that all men, aided by the illumining light of the Spirit, can comprehend the truth. "The Scriptures, therefore, are plain and perspicuous in all things necessary to salvation, and adapted to the instruction even of the most unlearned, through the medium of diligent and constant reading." Hence Milton excerpted from the *Bible* for his own good these hundreds of texts, which he arranged and connected in such a way as to form what he called his "Christian doctrine." The same task he urged on all others who would hold a true faith. And that every one might be free to do this, Milton was ready to grant a wide toleration, at least to believers, for he realized that independent thinking must result in diversity of opinion. This, in brief, was Milton's attitude toward the *Bible*, an attitude that explains both the existence of *Christian Doctrine* and the Scriptural basis of the epics.

It may at first seem impossible to reconcile the extremely literal reading of the *Bible*, which is the foundation of *Christian Doctrine*, and the poetic interpretation found in parts of *Paradise Lost*. The visions of the poet, we suspect, often outstripped the reasoning of the theologian. In an early poem he speaks of the soul after death as carrying on its high existence, not altogether dissociated from this world and its inhabitants; his words are:

> Or unsphere
> The spirit of Plato, to unfold
> What worlds or what vast regions hold
> The immortal mind that hath forsook
> Her mansion in this fleshly nook.

But in *Christian Doctrine* he proves, to his own satisfaction, that souls have no existence between death and Judgment Day. Doubtless, he became more of a theologian in the time intervening between the composition of *Il Penseroso* and *Chris-*

tian Doctrine; for much Puritan teaching told him to accept all Biblical statements as of equal value, and controversy forced him to stand rigidly. But there was the more liberal side to his nature, and in *Paradise Lost* he shows the poet's, not the theologian's, judgment.

Although *Christian Doctrine* and *Paradise Lost* may rest on the same foundation, the *Bible*, there is this vital difference between them. The prose work contains simply a cold statement and exegesis of hundreds of Scriptural texts; the epic embodies in transfigured form whatever is most essential in this body of doctrine for the elucidation of God's ways to man. Nothing will exemplify the difference more plainly than a comparison of the chapter on the creation in *Christian Doctrine* with the seventh book of the epic. In one, Milton gives, with ample substantiation from Scripture, his beliefs regarding the creation of the universe and man. He declares that God created the world by his word and spirit; that Christ was the "less principal cause" of creation; that the world was not created out of nothing, and that matter, therefore, can not be annihilated; that the apostasy of the angels occurred before the creation; that pre-existence of the soul is not mentioned in the *Bible;* and that the soul is not created at birth by special act of God. Almost all of these propositions can be found somewhere in *Paradise Lost*, but without accompanying argument. The exact thought of *Christian Doctrine* is expressed in the lines:

> The King of Glory, in his powerful Word
> And Spirit coming to create new worlds,

and

> But on the watery calm
> His brooding wings the Spirit of God outspread.[1]

But even where there is this close correspondence between the two works, the spirit is different. In one case Milton has a thesis to prove, in the other, an emotion to express. *Paradise Lost* presents a picture of creation, filled with the wonder of Job and the gratitude of the Psalmist. Milton displays his own warm remembrance of the glories of nature in such lines as,

> And sowed with stars the heaven thick as a field;

and in many more detailed pictorial passages he seems to remember the crude work of Du Bartas and the epithet-description of Virgil.[2] Such poetic elements in the narrative completely obscure its theological basis, and all is fused by the poet into a unified whole. As the description of creation reaches its close, in the work of the sixth day, the poet's emotion intensifies, and the spirits of earth and heaven burst forth, one grand, symphonic chorus in praise of their maker. The reader thinks, perhaps, of the close of *L'Allegro* and *Il Penseroso*, where the music of the lines rises with the thought to fine artistic climax; and the analogy is not inapt if it helps him to feel that this seventh book of the epic is no bare rehearsal of fact, but a hymn of praise.

[1] *P. L.*, 7, ll. 208–209, 234–235.   [2] See *P. L.*, 7, ll. 310 ff.

Such a study of *Paradise Lost* in its relation to *Christian Doctrine* and the *Bible* will inevitably remove part of the *onus* that the poem has of late been forced to bear. It is not a Calvinistic treatise, and God does not stand before the angels, as many have alleged, simply as an expositor of rigid Protestant theology. In the first place, Milton's belief is not Calvinistic, for he rejects the doctrines of predestination, the total depravity of man, and even the Trinity, in its strict form. Milton, in fact, is neither Calvinist nor Unitarian. In the second place, only those matters of doctrine are introduced that are necessary to Milton's main purpose — the justification of God's ways to man. The poem, therefore, displays not an outworn theology, but vital and enduring truths regarding man's place in this universe. It is the work of a man who has read the *Bible* with a poet's heart. Its story he accepts; its truth he perceives; its language and figures he almost unconsciously reproduces. No wonder, then, that *Paradise Lost* and *Paradise Regained* seem the highest examples of sacred poetry in English literature.

(b) *The Classics*

HOWEVER numerous the close correspondences between *Paradise Lost* and the *Bible* may be, English readers of culture have more often noted its relationship to the epics of Homer and Virgil. Addison, for example, asserts that "the thought of the golden compasses is conceived altogether in Homer's spirit," and fails to note that the direct source of Milton's idea is the poetical description of the creation in *Proverbs*. It is natural that the scholarly reader should thus at first regard the classics as the more important influence on Milton; for, whereas the *Bible* contributed many individual ideas and a countless number of words and phrases, the work of Homer and Virgil dictated the general form of the poem, as well as many details. Though Milton had once considered the poetry of the *Old* and *New Testaments* as not unfitting models for the modern poet, he eventually decided to cast his life's work in the mold of the classical epic.

The analysis of the epic structure of *Paradise Lost* that has already been made, shows how definitely the author had in mind the canons of Aristotelian criticism. He allowed himself the larger scope that the epic poet can claim, yet observed the principle of unity in this more comprehensive field. "With no middle flight" he soared to the height of the sublime, dealing with incidents marvelous and impossible, as Aristotle says that the epic poet may do. And, still following the tradition of the classical epic, he selected a theme in which the destiny of a whole people — indeed, in this case of a whole race — is involved. This phase of the epic is well explained by Butcher: "The epic poem relates a great and complete action, which attaches itself to the fortunes of a people, or to the destiny of mankind, and which sums up the life of a period." In all these essential respects, *Paradise Lost* is outwardly an imitation of the ancient epic.

But it is equally true that Milton adapted this universally accepted epic pattern and its minor conventions to suit his own purposes. His fixed intent was so to treat the theme he had selected as to render it most effective as a narrative and most fully expressive of his deepest thoughts. In so modifying the principles of the *Poetics*, he was influenced greatly by Tasso. But Tasso made his heroic poem a more slavish copy of the *Iliad* than Milton could consent to do. In variety of incident, in lack of emotional restraint, and in the frequent resort to the supernatural, *Jerusalem Delivered* resembles the medieval romance; but its framework and many of its incidents are strictly Homeric. Tasso, in the first place, recounts the story of a great war, waged for the capture of a foreign city. In this war the Italian knight, Rinaldo, plays a part similar to that of Achilles in the *Iliad;* for example, angered like Achilles through jealousy, Rinaldo abandons his allies, and their cause in consequence suffers. Tasso also enumerates, early in his poem, the various leaders of the Christian army, just as Homer catalogues the ships of the Greeks, and he attributes words of encouragement to Godfrey and Peter the Hermit that resemble the speeches of the Grecian leaders who urge a continuance of the war against Troy. Again, Erminia points out the Christian leaders to Aladine from the walls of Jerusalem, just as Helen names for Priam the Grecian generals seen from Troy's wall. And after the fashion of the pagan gods, Beelzebub assumes the shape of Clorinda to encourage the pagans to battle, and sends a dust storm to confuse the Christian army. Tancred and Argantes fight in single combat in imitation of Achilles and Hector, and everywhere the Homeric poem is in Tasso's mind. Milton, however, worked with much greater independence. He selected a "higher argument" than human deeds afford, and in its treatment, inspired by the nightly visitations of his "Celestial Patroness," he shaped his classical models to suit his ends.

This independence was forced upon Milton by the nature of the theme he had chosen and by his higher regard for Biblical history than for classical legend. Ancient mythology and history, he believed, are of value chiefly for what truth they mystically or by example reveal; in themselves they express no great truth. The *Bible*, on the contrary, gives the history of the race; for the Hebrews, as the Lord's chosen people, are the types of man in general. In the *Bible*, therefore, a modern nation like the English, destined, as Milton hoped, to enjoy in later times the divine favor that had once been granted the Hebrews, can find the salient truths of life. It would have been using a lower for a higher form of truth had he employed secular, rather than sacred, literature for the groundwork of his epic.   Both the form and the content of *Paradise Lost* were determined by the author's own carefully formulated purposes.

There are, notwithstanding, countless resemblances between Milton's poem and the classics. Addison noted many, as a man of wide reading; Todd, Bentley, and other editors have disclosed more;   and students of the scientific school of to-day have gathered others by close research. Just as in his early years the author of the Christian elegy, *Lycidas*, had employed all the conventions of the pagan elegy, so in *Paradise Lost* he adopted, for the conveyance of his deepest philosophy of life, both the general form and many of the details of the traditional epic.   This time-honored machinery of the epic is utilized in forms more or less modified to suit the new setting or the new purpose.   Incidents are alluded to or copied without acknowledgment in the building up of the narrative, and long epic figures, many of them directly borrowed from Homer and Virgil, serve to give amplification or color to the English poem. A person of Milton's training would have found it impossible to work otherwise in the epic form. To him, as to his learned contemporaries, the absence of epic conventions would have occasioned more surprise than their presence causes to-day.

Comment has already been made on the invocation with which *Paradise Lost* begins.   But the Heavenly Muse who is there addressed, is invoked again at the beginning of the seventh book, where the *locus* of the poem is changed from heaven to earth. In like manner, Virgil, at the beginning of the second half of the *Aeneid*, after the hero has returned from the realm of the dead, calls again to the heavenly guide, "Now come thou, Erato, and I will unfold what kings, what times, what modes of circumstance, — reigned in ancient Latium, when first the alien host ranged its barques on Ausonia's strand." Homer, too, makes several invocations in the *Iliad*.[1] Thus the opening of Milton's seventh book follows strictly classical precedent, and at the same time observes the higher law of artistic fitness; for the change of scene and spirit makes the renewal of the invocation very appropriate.

Possibly no other instance of epic convention in *Paradise Lost* has seemed to readers so incongruous as the account of the warfare in heaven. Milton's ultimate source for this is Hesiod's description in the *Theogony* of Zeus's battle with the Titans. Between the old and the new generations of gods in Grecian mythology existed the same antipathy as between God and Lucifer, and Zeus ordained "that whoso of the gods would fight with him against the Titans, none of them would he rob of his rewards." So Zeus, by showing kindness to the immortals of the younger generation, gathered his party about him. "Now do ye show," he admonished them, "against the Titans

[1] See *Iliad*, "Catalogue of Ships;" also, 11, l. 218; 16, l. 112.

in deadly fight both mighty force and hands invincible, in gratitude for our mild loving-kindness." They answered: "Excellent Lord, thou dost not tell things unlearnt by us: but we too are aware that thy wisdom is excellent, and excellent thine intellect, and that thou hast been to the immortals an averter of terrible destruction." Then Hesiod tells how the gods, "holding huge rocks in their sturdy hands," attacked the Titans, and how the sea and earth resounded and the heavens groaned. Finally, Zeus himself entered the battle, with fire and thunder. His followers fought behind him, "hurling from their sturdy hands three hundred rocks close upon each other." And so the Titans were conquered and hurled from Olympus to the depths of Tartarus, as far as heaven is from the earth, a distance that a falling anvil could traverse not under nine days and nights."[1] There, in the dark realm of Tartarus, inclosed by brazen gates and a strong wall, they are to dwell forever.

This story of combat between the gods finds place in *Paradise Lost*. Other details not given by Hesiod can be found in the *Iliad*. The single combat, for instance, between Michael and Lucifer is surely reminiscent of the fight between Achilles and Hector and of the whole seventeenth book of the *Iliad*.[2] The speeches, too, of *Paradise Lost* are modelled after those of Homer. And even such a minor detail as the flight of Moloch before

[1] See also, *Od.*, 11, ll. 315–316, and Hesiod's later description of the overthrow of Typhoeus.   [2] *Iliad*, 20, ll. 419–503.

Gabriel, reminds one of the defeat of Ares by Diomede.[1] "Then brazen Ares bellowed loud as nine thousand warriors or ten thousand cry in battle as they join in strife and fray," Homer tells us. Similarly, Milton shows how Moloch

> With shattered arms
> And uncouth pain, fled bellowing.

But Milton never would have been content to rest so long and so important a part of his epic on classical authority alone. Although the *Theogony* has been called the ultimate source of this episode, it must not be forgotten that in *Jude* and *Revelation* the war is briefly mentioned; that those same sources authorize the part played by Michael in the sixth book; and that even details like the hurling of the hills are suggested in the *Bible* as well as by Hesiod. And as Milton rises to the climax of his story, when Christ rides forth in person to overthrow the champion of evil, Milton turns again to the *Bible*. His splendid picture of the Savior riding forth in the heavenly chariot was taken from the dream of the prophet Ezekiel. Even the sixth book of *Paradise Lost*, therefore, seemingly so ultra-classical in content, shows what a composite the epic really is. The account of the war between God and Lucifer rests primarily on the *Theogony* and the *Bible*; it borrows also largely from the *Iliad* and *Aeneid*; and then, for its climax, has recourse again to the

[1] *Iliad*, 5, ll. 859–861. See Himes, p. 380.

pages of the *Bible*. In this respect the sixth book
of the poem is thoroughly characteristic of its
cultured Puritan author.

Closely dependent though this portion of *Paradise Lost* may be on the older epics, Milton handles
his material in his own individual way. Homer is
interested in each detail of the combat for its own
sake, and states facts as facts. Milton, on the
contrary, weaves the details together into magnificent pictures, and values them chiefly, it seems,
for their pictorial qualities. The description of
Satan's recoil, for example, has the magnitude of
some great mural painting:

> So saying, a noble stroke he lifted high,
> Which hung not, but so swift with tempest fell
> On the proud crest of Satan that no sight,
> Nor motion of swift thought, less could his shield,
> Such ruin intercept. Ten paces huge
> He back recoiled; the tenth on bended knee
> His massy spear upstayed: as if, on earth,
> Winds under ground, or waters forcing way,
> Sidelong had pushed a mountain from his seat,
> Half-sunk with all his pines.

Other pictures are full of sound and movement.

> Now storming fury rose,
> And clamour such as heard in Heaven till now
> Was never; arms on armour clashing brayed
> Horrible discord, and the madding wheels
> Of brazen chariots raged; dire was the noise
> Of conflict; overhead the dismal hiss
> Of fiery darts in flaming volleys flew,
> And, flying, vaulted either host with fire.
> So under fiery cope together rushed
> Both battles main with ruinous assault

> And inextinguishable rage.   All Heaven
> Resounded; and, had Earth been then, all Earth
> Had to her centre shook.

In these long descriptions, both the rapidity and the reality of Homer are lacking.   One may remember for its decorative art such a passage as:

> For likest gods they seemed,
> Stood they or moved, in stature, motion, arms,
> Fit to decide the empire of great Heaven.
> Now waved their fiery swords, and in the air
> Made horrid circles; two broad suns their shields
> Blazed opposite, while Expectation stood
> In horror; from each hand with speed retired,
> Where erst was thickest fight, the Angelic throng,
> And left large field, unsafe within the wind
> Of such commotion.

But the episode seems remote from earthly conflict — a struggle in which greater, but less tangible, than human interests are at stake.

Milton asserts his own individuality, also, by infusing into the narrative a strong moral undercurrent.   The battle brought into heaven "deformed rout" and "foul disorder"; the din of war was "odious."   Nor is the thought forgotten that all may be but a symbol.   The angel who brings the narrative to Adam explains that he has described these marvels in terms of human experience, implying that such a conflict is only man's way of conceiving the irreconcilable enmity between good and evil.   Angels, indeed, might find other words and other symbols to express it.   But the nature of the symbol is of no moment, if only it serves to warn man of the presence of his

arch foe and the need of circumspection. The
final impression, therefore, that the book should
leave with the reader is of the creative power of
its author. He has given the old incidents a new
setting; he has infused into them a new feeling.
Again he exhibits the powers of assimilation and
creation working in perfect unison.

Other incidents are transposed from the classics
to *Paradise Lost* with less modification and less
thorough assimilation, because their importance
in Milton's general scheme is less. One detail,
indeed, from the *Theogony* seems ill-fitted to its
new setting. In Tartarus, Hesiod continues, after
telling of the Titans' defeat, dwell Sin and
Death, and, in front of the mansion of Pluto and
Persephone, watches the ruthless dog, Cerberus,
who "devours whomsoever he may have caught
going forth without the gates." This fiction was
in Milton's mind when he described Sin and
Death as the gate-keepers of Satan's prison-
house. Sin is seated at the portal, while

> About her middle round
> A cry of Hell-hounds never-ceasing barked
> With wide Cerberean mouths full loud, and rung
> A hideous peal.

That God should have entrusted the keys of Hell
to these guards, with strict injunction against
opening the gates, seems hardly conceivable; for
Sin and Death, instead of wishing to keep Satan
and the other evil spirits in captivity, would wel-
come their escape. The incongruity is due to the

two-fold source from which the conception is drawn. By identifying Satan with that lust which is mentioned by James as the origin of all sin, Milton derives the idea of Satan's progeny from the verse, "Then when lust hath conceived, it bringeth forth sin: and sin, when it is finished, bringeth forth death." In visualizing these abstractions, Milton's mind recurred to the legend of the *Theogony;* Sin and Death become persons, and their abode necessarily is hell. All this is fitting; but the intrusion of the legend of Cerberus into the picture renders it incongruous. Still, if hell were to have any guards, they must needs be faithless to their trust, else Satan never could have reached Eden. Satan's sin-born progeny, therefore, may after all be as fit as any for the duty imposed.

Other less conspicuous incidents in *Paradise Lost* can be traced exclusively to classical sources. The debate in hell, in which the future policy of Satan and his followers is determined, corresponds to the council scene in the second book of the *Iliad*, where the first impulse of the Achæans to abandon the war is overcome, and the leaders decide to continue the struggle. The games in hell, likewise, with which the fallen angels amuse themselves after the adjournment of the council, remind one of the games of the Greeks after the burial of Patroklos and those of the Romans in memory of Anchises. But Homer and Virgil are interested in the details of the chariot races and

other contests of skill and strength for their own
sake; Homer, especially, was near in time to the
civilization in which such things bulked large.
With Milton, however, the case is different; he
cares nothing for such diversion and employs it
simply as an epic convention. The contestants,
also, in the deeds of physical strength interest him
less than those more intellectual spirits who re-
tire to sing or to converse on weighty themes; for
here he can show how vain are the harmonies of
the apostates, who, instead of God and his glory,
have only "their own heroic deeds and hapless
fall" to celebrate, and how futile is the effort to
fathom the workings of divine providence for those
who have lost its inner light. In the wanderings
of other spirits through the precincts of hell, Milton finds opportunity, also, to describe, more fully
than he has done before, the exact topography of
the region. In this way Milton welds firmly in
the general scheme of his poem the incidents that
he borrows from the classics.

It goes almost without saying that the amount
of matter so borrowed from Grecian and Roman
literature must vary from book to book. If the
account of the conflict in heaven rests to a very
considerable extent on a classical foundation, the
revelation to Adam of the future destiny of the
race depends even more exclusively on sacred history. The story of creation, likewise, is based
largely on the *Bible*. But here there is opportunity for description that the closing books of

the poem do not afford, and these descriptions abound with pictorial details suggested by Homer and Virgil. So even where incidents can not be transposed, Milton finds enrichment for his epic pictures in classical sources.

Correspondences such as these are too numerous to be listed. The movement of the hosts of heaven is compared by Milton to the assembling of birds in Eden to receive their names. So Homer likens the gathering of Grecian warriors to the "many tribes of feathered birds, wild geese, or cranes or long-necked swans, on the Asian mead, by Kaystrios' stream," who "fly hither and thither joying in their plumage, and with loud cries settle ever onwards, and the mead resounds." [1] Virgil employs the same figure thus: "They marched in even measure and sang of their king: as often snowy swans in the moist clouds, when full-fed they return." [2] So the angels are said to lie in hell "entranced, thick as autumnal leaves that strow the brooks," just as Homer compares the generations of men to the leaves of the trees that fall and die before the new buds come, or as Virgil compares the crowd gathering on the river bank to "the leaves that fall in the forest at the first chill breath of autumn." [3] The bare simile,

> As, when heaven's fire
> Hath scathed the forest oaks or mountain pines,

[1] *Iliad*, 2, ll. 459 ff.
[2] *Aeneid*, 7, ll. 699 ff.
[3] *Iliad*, 6, l. 146; *Aeneid*, 6, l. 309.

revives Homer's frequent pictures of the ravaging fire. Such comparisons, in fact, are usually reminiscent of no one passage. The swarming of the bees, which Milton uses to describe the movements of the fallen angels, has its counterpart in both the *Iliad* and the *Aeneid*, and the figure of the ravening wolf might have been suggested either by the *Iliad* or the *Bible*.[1]

Descriptive words and phrases are borrowed in the same apt way. Bentley called attention to the correspondence between Milton's "right red hand" and Horace's "rubente dextra." Newton connected "ignoble ease" with Virgil's "ignobilis oti." The beautiful phrase, "labouring moon," is to be found in the *Georgics* and Juvenal's satires, and the exact phrase, "the gods who live at ease," is found in Homer. Milton also translates literally Homer's epithet for Hesperus, "fairest of stars," and borrows directly from the same source such transitions as:

> Now Night her course began, and, over heaven
> Inducing darkness, grateful truce imposed.

In general, one of Milton's favorite and most effective means of description was the adjective, and many of his most apt adjectival phrases are derived directly from classical literature.

So frequent are these borrowings that Milton's thought seems to be often only a composite of ideas derived from classical poetry. Professor Os-

[1] *Iliad*, 2, l. 87; 12, l. 167; *Aeneid*, 1, l. 430; 6, l. 707.

good has analyzed clearly one such passage in *Paradise Lost:* [1]

> All night the dreadless Angel, unpursued,
> Through Heaven's wide champaign held his way, till Morn,
> Waked by the circling Hours, with rosy hand
> Unbarred the gates of Light.   There is a cave
> Within the Mount of God, fast by his throne,
> Where Light and Darkness in perpetual round
> Lodge and dislodge by turns — which makes through Heaven
> Grateful vicissitude, like day and night;
> Light issues forth, and at the other door
> Obsequious Darkness enters, till her hour
> To veil the heaven, though darkness there might well
> Seem twilight here.

"In this passage," Professor Osgood states, "there is an almost literal adaptation of at least four classical poets or poetic conceptions. The general idea of Dawn's opening the gates is from Ovid; the action of the Hours is from Homer; the cave of Light and Darkness is Hesiod's house of Day and Night; the final rout of Night before the beams of the sun is a common conception in Greek poetry, though perhaps in this case referable to Dante."   It would pay to follow this analysis further, but the composite nature of Milton's epic may have been already sufficiently illustrated.

The same writer has also shown most sympathetically the use Milton makes of classical mythology.[2]   In some cases Milton introduces his allusions in the form of similes and metaphors, often grouping several together for their cumulative

[1] Osgood, *Classical Mythology of Milton's English Poems,* p. xxvii.
[2] *Ibid.,* pp. xiii ff.

effect. Besides this method, which is noticeable especially in the epics and *Comus*, Milton in many places incorporates some myth in an original setting. For example, Chaos, which is but vaguely and briefly treated by classical poets, is fully elaborated in *Paradise Lost;* and Eve experiences just the same surprise that befell Narcissus. Or, in the third place, mythology is employed to give color to descriptions of nature. In general, Milton's use of classical myth shows not slavish borrowing, but a "beautiful synthesis" of ideas gathered from a number of sources. Out of this dependence on the classics came the poet's growing freedom from the oddities of Caroline poetry and his surer taste. On the whole, Professor Osgood concludes, Milton in the treatment of classical mythology exhibits both the range and the inclusiveness of his reading.

To handle this one phase of ancient thought in so scholarly a way, Milton must have possessed a thorough knowledge of classical literature. In all his poetry, as indeed in his prose as well, such knowledge is visible. The two epics display the most sympathetic familiarity with the poetry of Hesiod, Homer, and Virgil. *Samson Agonistes* is carefully modelled after the pattern of Grecian tragedy. *Comus* is filled with the philosophical idealism of Plato; for even its tribute to the power of chastity and the supremacy in general of soul over body, is as much the result of Platonic as of Christian teaching. Likewise, the *Tractate on*

Education shows direct influence from Xenophon and Plutarch. Milton's classicism should not be judged by his readiness to quote from ancient literature in his prose tracts; for such excerpts were then commonly gathered by controversialists totally destitute of any sense of literary values. In such display of erudition, a pedant as stupid as "marginal Prynne" easily outranked the true scholar and poet who contemptuously gave him the nickname. Milton's classicism is of a higher sort. In the *Tractate on Education* he outlines a thorough course of classical study designed to quicken a boy's thought and give him the information and the power of expression that he needs. Such was the benefit that he himself had derived from antiquity. The poets and philosophers of Greece and Rome, and their historians and scientists, had all contributed in turn to the mental development of the poet. All, too, had done something to mold his character and ideals. To estimate completely Milton's debt to the classics will remain an impossible task—a task for the philologian, the grammarian, the student of literature and philosophy, and the psychologist.

Nevertheless, broad as the problem is, it has seemed not unfair to confine this analysis of Milton's classicism to *Paradise Lost*. Better than any other poem, this great epic represents all phases of Milton's indebtedness to the classics. Its general form was patterned after the *Iliad* and the *Aeneid;* many of its episodes come directly from

the same sources; and much of its phraseology is
of classical origin. *Comus* shows some of these
same influences, but is more strongly tinged with
romantic elements. *Samson Agonistes* is an even
closer copy than the epic of a classical pattern,
but its spirit and content are purely Hebraic. In
regard to this play the problem would be to determine how much the thought and spirit of the
Attic playwrights modified Milton's Hebraism.
More adequately than any other of his poems,
Paradise Lost displays his wide reading in classical
literature. It is one of the most classical, as it is
one of the most Biblical, poems in our literature.

(c) *The Italian Renaissance*

THIS analysis of the direct influence of the classics upon *Paradise Lost* must be supplemented by
a discussion of the indirect classical influence that
came to Milton through the literature of the Italian Renaissance. Just as the drama of Tudor
humanists was strongly affected by Italian plays,
so the definition of epic poetry that prevailed in
the seventeenth century shows plainly the effects
of Italian criticism. A restatement in enlarged
form of the Aristotelian theory of heroic poetry
was forced upon Italian critics by the popularity
of the romance, a form of poetry that violated all
accepted principles of criticism and yet for its
popularity seemed to deserve official sanction.
Some orthodox critics were inclined to censure the
romance. Trissino, for example, disapproved of

the *Orlando Furioso* for its lack of unity, and, in slavish imitation of Homer, composed the *Italia Liberata* to show what the true heroic poem should be. But Giraldi Cintio, Pigna, and others were ready to defend the romance, although they acknowledged its want of unity in plot. Finally, Minturno assumed a compromise position, admitting that the varied and improbable subject-matter of the romances was legitimate for poetry, but objecting to their formlessness. This line of argument was carried further by Tasso, who in several critical treatises expounded the theory of heroic poetry, and in *Jerusalem Delivered* sought to prove that a true epic may possess all the variety of the romance and yet retain structural unity. Into this long and at times acrimonious debate, the best minds of the time were drawn, and no serious student of literature could remain in ignorance of the general trend of the controversy.

This, however, was not Milton's only point of contact with the poetry of modern Italy; for he was widely read in the best Italian literature. The scenes of enchantment in *Comus* owe something to the direct influence of Ariosto, and not everything to the indirect influence that came from the Italian through Spenser. Milton quotes, also, from Ariosto in *Reformation in England*, and translates literally from *Orlando Furioso* the much discussed phrase, "things unattempted yet in prose or rhyme." Furthermore, *Lycidas* accepts in part the innovations of the Italian elegiac poets; and the sonnets, both in Italian and English, reveal indisputable evidence of Petrarchan study. One might expect to find even stronger bonds of connection between Milton and Dante; but this is hardly the case. Milton alludes to the *Divine Comedy* in the sonnet addressed to Henry Lawes, and quotes from it in one of his prose works. His phrase, "sphere of Fortune," has also been traced to Dante's poem, and numerous other correspondences between the two poets' works have been cited.[1] But in general the influence of Dante was of a sort that can not be measured or even traced, and Pommrich is justified in asserting that Tasso left the most visible impress on Milton's poetic development. The reason for this, and his whole connection with Italian letters, can best be explained by reference to a few details of his life.

Very early in life Milton began the study of the Italian language. In the poem, *Ad Patrem*, he speaks gratefully of the opportunity afforded him in youth of mastering Italian, and the assumption is not unwarranted that he had read Fairfax's translation of Tasso's epic even before he was able to understand it in the original. To this study Milton was naturally encouraged by the interest of his closest friend, Charles Diodati, the son of an Italian refugee then resident in London. Consequently, by the year 1638 when he visited Italy,

[1] See C. G. Osgood, *M. L. N.*, 22, pp. 140–141, and O. Kuhns, *Ibid.*, 13, pp. 1–12.

he was fully prepared to meet the most gifted literary men of Florence, Naples, and Rome. In Florence, he was hospitably entertained by Mansus, who had been the friend and benefactor of Tasso; and at Rome he was fortunate in making the acquaintance of Lucas Holstenius, the papal secretary. Milton's Italian sonnets, which presumably were composed during this period of travel, beautifully attest his command of the language, and indicate, also, his preference for the so-called Petrarchan sonnet form. In these Italian poems, one sees again that rare combination of knowledge and creative power that distinguishes all Milton's great work.

Of all the Italian poets Tasso seems to have appealed to Milton most strongly. Pommrich finds much in Tasso's sad life and in his nobility of character that would rouse Milton's interest and sympathy. In addition, Milton's cordial host, Mansus, presumably recommended most warmly to the attention of his guest the work of the great poet he had once befriended. It is not surprising, therefore, that Milton, who so seldom mentions modern poets by name, should refer four times to Tasso, twice in the letter to Mansus, again, in connection with the singer, Leonora Baroni, and, lastly, in his remarks on the nature of the epic poem.[1] This last reference is of especial importance, because it was written very shortly after

[1] *Ad Mansum*, "Introduction" and ll. 7, 50; *Ad Eandem* (Leonoram); *Ch. Gov.*, 2, p. 478.

the author's Italian journey and is directly related to the composition of *Paradise Lost*. This
alone justifies our giving to Tasso the place of
first importance among the Italian poets.

It was due in large measure to Tasso's influence
that Milton first planned to give epic form to the
great poem that he early aspired to write, and that
his thoughts were turned, as he sought a subject,
to early English history. Tasso had insisted that
the epic poet should choose a theme involving the
large interests of his own country, and the heroism
of some great national leader. The story, also,
should not be too ancient to engage the warm
interest of the poet's contemporaries, nor too
modern to warrant heroic treatment. As suiting
all these requirements, the critic mentions the
legends of Charlemagne and Arthur. How significant, then, seems Milton's remark in addressing
Tasso's patron, Mansus, that he is meditating a
great poem — evidently from his description an
epic — on the Arthurian legend or some other
story from early British history. Milton soon
abandoned this first intention, owing to his regard for Biblical story. But the theme that he
finally selected, according to his own interpretation, had a really national significance, and gave
opportunity for the display of heroism in which
the modern Englishman could feel sympathy.
Tasso had also insisted that the modern epic should
be Christian in subject and teaching; since the
marvelous incidents of the epic are credible only

if they are attributed to a deity in whom its readers can have faith, and since the hero's perfection of character is possible only in a Christian. So Milton's epic deals with a Christian theme, which has also a real bearing on English life, yet is not so deeply involved in dogma as to hamper his invention as a poet. In all essential respects, Milton's *Paradise Lost* meets the requirements for the heroic poem that Tasso's critical essays prescribe.

Tasso would have approved the long deliberation that Milton gave to his choice of subject; for the critic, in one of his essays, calls that the first step in the creation of an epic poem. As the second step he names the giving of artistic form to the matter selected. In this, Milton was little influenced by Italian theory or example, for he followed the better model of the ancient poets and his own sure sense of form. But in the third test to which the epic poet must submit, the addition of poetic adornment to the bare theme, Milton's debt to Tasso was certainly greater. Nevertheless, although many similarities between Milton's epic and Tasso's have been pointed out, the question of their relationship is still unsettled.[1]

Unquestionably, there are passages in *Jerusalem Delivered* that remind an English reader of *Paradise Lost*. Satan, for example, filled with jealousy

[1] See Pommrich, E., Miltons Verhältnis zu Torquato Tasso.   Halle, 1902.

and hate as he watches the victorious advance
of the Christian army, summons his followers to a
council of war, and, by reminding them of their
former glory, urges them to resist the advancing
Crusaders either by force or fraud. Again,
Michael, who in *Paradise Lost* leads the assault
on Satan's host, is sent to drive back the devils
to hell. Another detail, the entrance of the
Egyptian army into Jerusalem by an underground
passage, may bring to mind Satan's mode of entering Eden. Finally, Michael appears to Godfrey
and, removing the film from his eyes, reveals the
angelic hosts that are marshalled to fight in his
defense. This, too, has its counterpart at the close
of the English epic. And in addition to these
larger correspondences, Pommrich discovers many
resemblances in detail, more or less convincing.
In Fairfax's translation of Tasso, for instance,
hell is called the "house of grief and pain," while
in *Paradise Lost* it is called "the house of woe and
pain." Furthermore, both Tasso and Milton liken
the number of the fallen angels to the leaves that
strew the ground in autumn. Many other such
details might easily be added.

But this evidence offers no very convincing
proof of indebtedness on Milton's part. Each poet,
to be sure, describes a conclave in hell; but Milton's takes place immediately after the fall of
Lucifer, and Tasso's occurs during the Crusades.
Such councils of war, it may be added, have been
common in epic poetry, and this and the other

points of similarity noted above can be accounted
for better than by assuming any direct borrowing
from Tasso. Milton found Michael designated in
Revelation as the leader of the angelic host against
the rebels in heaven; in the *Iliad* and the *Aeneid*
he found revelations of the future, given the hero
by supernatural means. Nor do the verbal resemblances warrant the assumption of close copy-
ing on Milton's part. It would be hazardous to
assert that no recollection of Tasso's language was
in the mind of the blind poet as he composed;
for his memory was a veritable storehouse of
treasures from the world's literature. But the
phrases that he seemingly took from Tasso had
become part of his own possession, with only a
subconscious realization of their source left in his
mind. Tasso's influence on Milton can never be
judged merely by listing such parallelisms.

This conclusion does not undervalue the rich
gifts inherited by Milton from the works of Tasso
and the other Italian poets. After all, a poet does
not reveal his actual indebtedness to his predecessors in verbal borrowings. The vital influence
of the Renaissance went to the upbuilding of Milton's poetic life. Dante's vision of the unseen
world must have done much to inspire the Puritan
poet in *Paradise Lost*. Tasso contributed vitally
to the quickening and enrichment of Milton's
mind, as he certainly aided him in the formation
of a sound theory of epic poetry. Milton's sonnets in English and Italian are the fruits of Pe-

trarch's example. Just how much these Italian
forces counted in the development of Milton's
powers, the world can never know; Milton himself did not know. The poet Wordsworth, whose
temperament was formed by forces singularly few
and easily defined, does not give an altogether
satisfactory account of his mental growth. And
Milton surely could not tell just how much he was
indebted to this influence or that for his varied gifts.
But he would have counted his knowledge of Italian
poetry one of the most priceless of his possessions.

(d) *English Poetry*

DURING the foregoing examination of the foreign
sources of *Paradise Lost*, it is to be hoped that
the reader has kept in mind the discussion of
Milton's relationship to the Elizabethans. Otherwise, the misapprehension might arise that Milton
was an exotic spirit among the Caroline poets,
owing little to the literature of his native land.
Even the slightest acquaintance, however, with
his scholarly and literary interests would forbid
such an assumption; his pride in England's history and his high hope for her future would cooperate with his general intellectual curiosity to
lead him to a knowledge of English letters. He
may apparently prefer the classics; for they, more
nearly than many of the unproved works of English authors, approached high, absolute standards of art. The satires of Hall, for example,
meant nothing to him in comparison with Juve-

nal's; the trifling conceits and amorous fancies of
contemporary song writers seemed to degrade the
high calling of Aeschylus or Virgil.   But the best
of Chaucer, Spenser, and Shakespeare — in fact,
whatever English thought seemed "not of an age
but for all time," was known and rightly valued
by Milton.

Writing in youth when the impulse from the
Elizabethan Age was strongest, Milton recorded
in several interesting passages his sympathetic
recollections of earlier English poetry.   He speaks
of Chaucer's unfinished story of Cambuscan, and,
in an allusion to Spenser too apt to be mistaken,
mentions other romantic tales,

> Of turneys, and of trophies hung,
> Of forests, and enchantments drear,
> Where more is meant than meets the ear.

In *L'Allegro* he gives one of the most just
comparisons ever drawn between Jonson and
Shakespeare:

> Then to the well-trod stage anon,
> If Jonson's learned sock be on,
> Or sweetest Shakespeare, Fancy's child,
> Warble his native wood-notes wild.

This fine bit of poetical criticism and his poem on
Shakespeare, printed in 1632 in the Second Folio
edition of the plays, amply prove his open admiration of the dramatist.   And if the lines on the
theater in the *First Elegy*, written though they
are in classical terms, may be taken in conjunc-
tion with the lines of *Il Penseroso*,

Or what (though rare) of later age
Ennobled hath the buskined stage,

there will be reason to believe that Milton was
familiar with Shakespeare's contemporaries as
well. Milton's literary taste, then, was not wholly
a product of the schools.

Less frequent and less apposite are the allusions
to English authors in the prose pamphlets of the
middle period of Milton's career. But it is significant that English works are sometimes quoted,
side by side with classical authorities, in support
of his arguments. To this end Milton mentions
"The Vision and Creed of Pierce Plowman" as a
powerful satire, and cites a passage from Gower
as an example of "truth delivered of old by a
voice from heaven." At this time, to be sure,
instead of speaking, as he once had done, of Chaucer's romantic tales, he uses the words of the Friar
to uncover the evils of confession, and the
words of the simple Ploughman to condemn the
pride of bishops.[1] And in *Eikonoklastes*, to prove
that fair words in an evil king are not to be relied
on, Milton quotes the hypocritical professions of
Shakespeare's Richard III. So to subpoena the
Father of English Poetry and the greatest of
dramatists and wrest from them unwilling testimony in behalf of the Puritan cause, seems a
perversion of *belles-lettres*. But that one hears
nothing more of Chaucer as a master of romance
or of Shakespeare as Fancy's child, is no proof

[1] *Apology*, 3, pp. 141, 164; *Reform.*, 2, pp. 390, 396.

that Milton had lost his youthful love for pure literature. On the contrary, these citations indicate that, even in the hurry and bitterness of party strife, Milton still looked to the self-chosen studies of his youth.

This present chapter, however, is to deal only with those English works to which *Paradise Lost* stands closely related. Of these, the Biblical paraphrase often attributed to Caedmon deserves first consideration.[1] Historically, there appears to be no evidence that Milton was acquainted with this Old English version of *Genesis*. The manuscript, to be sure, rested in London in the library of Archbishop Usher from 1640, or thereabouts, till 1650; but there is no reason to believe that Milton knew of its existence, or that he could have deciphered it even had he chanced to see it. About the middle of the century, however, the manuscript was given by its owner to the foreign scholar, Junius, who appears to have taken it with him when he left England shortly afterwards. In 1655 a reprint of the poem was issued in Amsterdam, and some copies of the edition doubtless reached London. At the time, Milton was already blind, and, since the book contained no translation or comment, it seems hardly likely that any one of his friends, when English philology was so little understood, would have been able to read or translate the poem for him. It is of course possible that Junius himself, during his residence

[1] See above pp. 87–88, 102–106.

in London, read portions of the old poem to the busy pamphleteer; but this is mere conjecture, warranted by no real correspondence between *Paradise Lost* and this earlier version of Lucifer's fall, the creation of the world, and the sin of Adam. The parallelisms between the two are easily accounted for by the common traditions from which both poets drew their material, and the differences, to which attention has already been called, are marked. We believe that Milton knew of Caedmon only Bede's brief reference, which is described in the *Common-Place Book* as a "pleasant little story of an English poet suddenly made such by divine inspiration." [1]

It is generally agreed that a closer connection with *Paradise Lost* has been proved for Sylvester's translation of Du Bartas' *La Semaine* and its sequel. There is, in the first place, interesting bibliographical evidence that this old folio would naturally be one of the first books to come to Milton's attention. Sylvester's complete translation of Du Bartas was published in 1605–6 by Humphrey Lownes on Bread Street, where Milton was born in 1608. The elder Milton, who like his neighbor was a book-lover and Puritan, must have known Lownes, and *The Diuine Weekes and Workes* would doubtless be brought into his home. In support of this conjecture, Dunster

[1] S. v. Gajšek assumes that Milton knew the old poem. *Milton und Caedmon*, Wien, 1911. Gurteen gives the best analysis and comparison.

cites from Milton's early poem, *The Passion*, as a possible reference to Sylvester's quarto of 1613, the lines:

> The leaves should all be black whereon I write,
> And letters, where my tears have wash'd, a wannish white.

This conceit, it is alleged, has reference to the elegy, included in that particular edition of *The Diuine Weekes and Workes*, in memory of Prince Henry. One of the two title-pages of this poem is a white leaf with a black back; the other is a black sheet, printed with letters that Dunster describes as "wannish white." Partly on this bibliographical evidence he would believe that *The Diuine Weekes and Workes* was one of the first books with which Milton was acquainted — the Prima Stamina, as he calls it, of *Paradise Lost*.

In addition to such bibliographical data, there is also persuasive internal evidence of this relationship. Milton's translations of Psalms 114 and 115, which are his earliest extant poems, contain a great deal of Sylvester's phraseology. A still more significant resemblance is found in these lines of *At a Vacation Exercise*:

> Yet I had rather, if I were to choose,
> Thy service in some graver subject use,
> Such as may make thee search thy coffers round,
> Before thou clothe my fancy in fit sound:
> Such where the deep transported mind may soar
> Above the wheeling poles, and at Heaven's door
> Look in, and see each blissful deity.

Dunster compares this whole passage with Sylvester's lines:

> And though our soul live as imprisoned here
> In our frail flesh, and buried, as it were,
> In a dark tomb, yet at one flight she flies
> From Calpe to Imaus, from th' earth to skies,
> Much swifter than the chariot of the sun, . . .
> She mounts above the world's extremest wall,
> Far, far beyond all things corporeal,
> Where she beholds her Maker, face to face,
> His frowns of justice and his smiles of grace;
> The faithful God, the chaste and sober port,
> And sacred pomp of the celestial court.

Another pertinent quotation would be:

> Then should I fly with Eagles' wings
> Unto the glorious King of Kings;
> And see that Heav'nly Court of his
> The Beauty of the Angels' Blisse. [1]

Such comparisons as these strongly confirm the evidence from other sources that Milton in youth was familiar with Sylvester's translations.

But it is hard to believe that *Paradise Lost* is dependent in any measurable degree on *The Divine Weekes and Workes*. There are, to be sure, thoughts and phrases common to both. Du Bartas supposes that Chaos is ruled by the four elements, hot, cold, moist, and dry. On the authority of the Scriptures, he believes in the existence of waters above the firmament, and in describing Eden he amplifies the material furnished by *Genesis*. Or, as a moral philosopher, he argues on such abstract problems as the freedom of the will and the all-inclusiveness of Adam's sin. These matters find place in Milton's epic; but their presence is

[1] *Poems*, ed. Grosart, 1, pp. lii–liii; 2, p. 346.

due not to imitation of Sylvester but to the nature of the subject and the common knowledge of the time.   Even the verbal similarities adduced by Dunster show at most nothing more than an occasional sub-conscious recollection on Milton's part of his youthful reading.

With all the richest stores of the world's literature to inspire him, Milton could not have felt the need of assistance from a poet so inartistic and eccentric as Sylvester.   His verse is lumbering and uneven, and his unpolished diction is marred by strange compound words.   Sylvester's besetting sin, however, is verbosity — the unfortunate proneness to expand ideas that the world has forgotten.   Milton may never have accepted absolutely the discoveries of Copernicus; but he does not contemptuously array all his learning against them, as Sylvester does.   Nor does he argue at length on the existence of the waters above the firmament, or on Satan's assumption of the serpent form, or on the ability of the ark to accommodate all the passengers divinely provided for it. All these subjects and many more are grist for Sylvester's mill.   He discourses on the progress of the arts and the various diseases; he explains the inconveniences that have resulted from the ill-advised plans of the builders of Babel, and then proves that Hebrew is the most perfect language; he even stops to name the authors that have honored the various nations, naming More, Bacon, Sidney, and Elizabeth herself as the glories of

English letters. The difference between real art and such verbose display may be seen by a comparison of the last four lines of *Paradise Lost* with Sylvester's long account of the same incident, which he duly heralds in the margin as "an elegant comparison representing the lamentable condition of Adam and Eve driven out of Paradise." Though one grants willingly that Milton probably knew *The Diuine Weekes and Workes* in boyhood, it is impossible to believe that a poem so formless and inartistic had any vital influence upon him.

Sylvester need not even be credited with having led Milton to choose a Biblical theme. Tasso's inclination toward Christian poetry would carry more weight with Milton than anything Sylvester could say or do. And in the early seventeenth century many Biblical poems were composed in England and France. Drayton's *Moyses in a Map of Miracles*, Giles Fletcher's *Christ's Victorie and Triumph*, and Quarles' *Divine Poems*, all attest the esteem in which sacred poetry was then held.

Especial attention has recently been called to the work of Abraham Cowley for its supposed bearing on Milton.[1] In the year 1656, just after his return from France, Cowley published his *Davideis*, which he prefaced with an interesting discussion on the value and nature of true sacred

[1] Kirsten, R., *Studie über das Verhältnis von Cowley und Milton.* Leipzig, 1899.

poetry. He had evidently come to know, during his sojourn in France, Godeau's *Discours de la Poésie Chrestienne* and some of the French religious poems. In this essay Cowley reproaches modern poets for degrading their art in mere repetition of already out-worn legends or in celebration of wanton passion, when such an abundance of sacred history lay absolutely untouched. "Truth is truest Poesie," he declares, and he therefore recommends stories from the *Bible* for the poet's consideration. Kirsten asserts that the *Davideis* encouraged Milton to hasten to completion his great literary undertaking. But as early as 1642, in the *Reason of Church Government*, Milton had expressed his marked preference for a Biblical subject, and Cowley's late essay could have done little in directing Milton to a task on which his hopes had long been fixed, and for which he found such general approval.

To this already rapidly growing list of poems that have been called the sources of Milton's epics, Fletcher's *Christ's Victorie and Triumph* should be added, chiefly because of its relation to *Paradise Regained*. The patriotic narrative verse of Daniel and Drayton could next be tested. And it would not be idle to subject *Nosce Teipsum* to close scrutiny, for in at least one interesting passage Milton is known to have reproduced the psychology of Davies. In *Nosce Teipsum* the five organs of sense are said to transmit impressions to Fancy, which arranges and compares them. Then Fancy, "wit's looking glass," transmits the impressions so arranged to Wit, as Davies calls the understanding or judgment, where they are used in processes of abstract thought. This psychology is reproduced in the fifth book of *Paradise Lost*. But on more essential matters, as, for example, on the origin of the soul in man and the possibility of man's reattaining divine truth, Milton stands at odds with Davies. And so the study might go on, finding ever new connections in detail between Milton's thought or expression and that of other English poets, but ever ending with a conviction of the poet's true independence.

It is a relief, however, to turn from such minute study, whose results are at best fragmentary and usually quite inconclusive, to a consideration of the rich poetical inheritance that Milton derived from Spenser. "Milton was the poetical son of Spenser," Dryden declares in the Preface to the *Fables*, and then adds in justification of the remark, "Milton has acknowledged to me that Spenser was his original." Yet Spenser's influence upon Milton, owing to its nature, has been less discussed than that of a half dozen other authors. The relationship does not manifest itself most plainly in points that can be tabulated. Spenser reacted directly upon the spirit of Milton — arousing his interest, quickening his feeling, directing him to new channels of reading, especially in the Italian, and developing his power of expression. One would almost assert that Spenser, of all the English poets, contributed the most really vital forces to the growth of Milton's poetic life.[1]

Spenser and Milton were close akin in spirit and showed much the same sympathy for the two great forces of their times — humanism and Puritanism. Spenser lived when both movements in England were in their infancy. The *Shepherd's Calender* inaugurated the Elizabethan revival of the New Poetry, and the half-veiled allegory of several of its pastorals expresses the moderate Puritanism of Tudor days. Spenser's classicism, therefore, lacks the wide horizon and the surety of Milton's; it is appreciative, ardent, and beautifully expressed, but lacks the grasp and equipoise of later scholarship. His Puritanism, too, differs from Milton's in its mildness. In the *Shepherd's Calender* he denounces the greed and idle ease of the clergy, just as Milton does in *Lycidas*, and, it may be, speaks more pointedly against certain policies of church and state.[2] But his Puritanism is that of Grindal's time rather than Laud's, while as yet the conflict centered about vestments and church ceremonies, and still showed tolerance on "things indifferent." In both his Puritanism and his humanism Spenser was of an earlier generation than Milton.

Each poet had the true humanist's love of the

[1] Certain phases of Spenser's influence have been discussed above, pp. 29, 34.

[2] See Higginson, J. J., *Spenser's Shepherd's Calender*, N. Y., 1912; Padelford, F. M., *Spenser and the Puritan Propaganda*, Mod. Phil., 11, pp. 85–106.

æsthetic. Concerning his own temperament Milton wrote: "What besides God had resolved concerning me I know not, but this at least: he has instilled into me, if into any one, a vehement love of the beautiful." [1] "It is my habit day and night," he continues, "to seek for this idea of the beautiful, as for a certain image of supreme beauty, through all the forms and faces of things." Clearly, he would be a disciple of Plato. But Milton's love of the beautiful seems to be as much the product of an active mind as an emotion, whereas Spenser's appreciation of the beautiful is, like Keats', a passion which he does not fear to encourage. The intense glow of passion in the *Epithalamion*, compared with the calm statement just quoted from Milton's letter or the emotions displayed in *L'Allegro*, marks the vital difference in temperament of these two kindred poets. In the same way, the sensuous appeals to carnal instinct that Guyon, Spenser's Knight of Temperance, has to face, contrast very strongly with the cold and repulsive temptations that the Lady in *Comus* overcomes. There is in Spenser little of Milton's intellectual equipoise and Hebraic severity.

Yet Spenser felt just as keenly as Milton did the moral responsibilities of life. Guyon, as a knight in the world of romance, serves the same ideal of temperance and morality that Milton set for himself in Cambridge and Italy, and that he

[1] See above, p. 40.

upholds in *Comus*. Both poets held the same exalted idea of the duties of the clergy; both were
staunch supporters of the reformed church. Spenser's Puritanism, however, is softened by the
spontaneous ebullition of poetic feeling and passion; Milton's passion is always calmed, if not
fettered, by his intellectual and moral sense. Nevertheless, these are only external differences, and
Milton saw in Spenser a spirit akin to his own.

Of all Milton's poems, *Comus* and *Lycidas* exhibit the most unmistakable traces of Spenser's
influence. Details of plot and the machinery of
the supernatural in the one; passages of description, the attack on the clergy, and the whole
elegiac convention in the other; and some of the
phraseology of both, owe much to the *Shepherd's
Calender* and the *Faerie Queene*. This phase of the
question has already been discussed. Obviously,
neither Milton's epics nor *Samson Agonistes* could
be so directly influenced by Spenser. In selecting
the theme of *Paradise Lost* Milton purposely
turned away from the romantic world of the
Faerie Queene, and in organizing his poem he
obeyed more rigid structural principles than Spenser followed. Hence the *Bible*, the classics, and
the Renaissance epic are Milton's determining
sources. Of course, details from Spenser often
creep in. The phrase "adamantine chains" resembles Spenser's "chains of adamant." Both
poets ascribe the invention of gunpowder to Satan,
and give him the disguise of an old man. But

many more such resemblances might be adduced without vitiating the general conclusion that the Minor Poems are the most unmistakably Spenserian, and that in *Paradise Lost* other influences predominate.

The same may be said of the relation of *Paradise Lost* to English poetry in general. Milton's early poems were written before the old Elizabethan spirit was totally extinct in England, and, in many essential respects, they carry on the poetical traditions that their author had inherited from the past. Hence he is called "the last of the Elizabethans." Just as conspicuously, however, *Paradise Lost* is the product of another age; and the threads of connection between it and the immediate past are less noticeable. The English sources of Milton's epic are less important than those other sources here discussed.

(e) *Summary*

IT would be easy to add indefinitely to this list of books that may have influenced Milton in the composition of *Paradise Lost;* for, when Milton wrote, the story of Lucifer's revolt and Adam's fall had long been common property of theologians and poets. A lover of these "Quellen und Forschungen" hates to pass by Voltaire's interesting statement, made in 1727, that Milton had witnessed the performance of Andreini's *Adamo* in Milan, and had received from it his first thoughts of *Paradise Lost*. Equally interesting would be an

investigation of *Adamus Exsul;* for the great repu-
tation of Hugo Grotius and the personal visit
that Milton paid him in 1638, would almost inevitably bring the drama to the attention of the
young poet. To neither work does *Paradise Lost*
seem directly indebted. Even the contributions
of the notorious Lauder to the whole problem
have been forgotten, save by those who enjoy old
literary disputes or who are especially interested
in Dr. Johnson. But a third play, Vondel's
Lucifer, can not be dismissed with such cursory
attention. Its own merits as a poem, and the
claims that have been advanced for it as the
chief source of *Paradise Lost,* warrant fuller
consideration.

Vondel's drama, *Lucifer,* was first produced and
published in Amsterdam in 1654, two years after
Milton had become totally blind. But the immediate suppression of the play by the authorities in
Holland occasioned so much discussion that some
news of the event very probably reached Milton.
The poet's curiosity, which would naturally be
aroused, could be speedily gratified. In London
at that time, when close political and commercial
relations existed with Holland, some one could
have been found to read or translate the work to
the blind poet. Milton himself knew some Dutch;
for Roger Williams, during his residence in London
from 1651 to 1654, used to visit Milton to read
Dutch, in return for Milton's assistance in other
languages. Although the Rhode Island colonist's

letter enters into no further particulars, Masson suggests that Williams may have found time to read *Lucifer* to Milton before his final departure from London in the year of its publication. These facts go far to justify the assumption that Milton, in spite of his blindness, could have formed an acquaintance with the work of Vondel.

Two very thorough comparisons have been made by Englishmen in the effort to establish a connection between Milton's epic and Vondel's play. The investigation of Edmund Gosse is less thorough-going but more appreciative and sound than Mr. Edmundson's. The latter's radical conclusions virtually amount to the charge that Milton, not only in *Paradise Lost*, but in the second epic and in *Samson Agonistes* as well, borrows freely from Vondel's poems.

To establish this uncompromising position, Edmundson has collected every possible evidence, however minute, of borrowing on Milton's part. But too much can be made of accidental or seeming resemblances between the two poets' works. For instance, it might be assumed that Milton was guided by Vondel in choosing Adam and Samson as subjects for poems, did we not know that both were already under consideration as early as 1640. Hence it is possible for Masson to take a position diametrically opposed to Edmundson's. Although Masson is willing to admit that Milton may have known *Lucifer*, and even that Milton himself may have been acquainted with Dutch, he denies that

Milton borrowed from his contemporary. Most of the resemblances between the two poems, he emphatically asserts, are due to the traditional character of the subject they handle. In other cases, Milton has been made to appear a borrower by Edmundson's use of Milton's own language in the translation of the Dutch original. In still other cases, the slight resemblance is only accidental. To justify these assertions, Masson quotes from one of the ablest editors of Vondel, M. Van Lennep, the statement: "I do not regard it as proved that Milton was acquainted with Vondel or his tragedy." Masson's own conclusion is just as emphatic: "*Paradise Lost* would have been exactly the same as it is if Vondel's poems had never been written."

This would be the opinion of a reader acquainted with the general literature of the subjects handled by Milton and Vondel, but uninformed as to the results of such special studies as these under discussion. The two works are essentially different. Since one is an epic and the other a drama, they can not treat in the same way the two great episodes that they present. In addition, there are many accidental differences. Vondel places the creation of man before the defection of Lucifer, and assumes that the angels, even before the revolt, were mastered by evil inclinations. In general, the reader who is more concerned for the author's thought and purpose and poetic style than for merely verbal accidents, will probably accept

Masson's judgment, not feeling that he belittles
Vondel in so doing. His *Lucifer* is a great poem,
if not a great play, and would gain nothing were it
proved to be the source of Milton's epic.

So the search for possible sources of *Paradise
Lost* might go on. It has engaged the attention
of all students of Milton, from the spiteful Lauder,
who maliciously forged evidence to prove Milton
a "plagiary," to the most reverent of his editors.
In many byways of ancient and modern literature
reminders of *Paradise Lost* can be found. But
what do they indicate? Is it conscious borrowing
by Milton of ideas and forms of expression; or
unconscious employment of the fruits of early
reading and study; or simply the reappearance in
different places of thoughts naturally pertaining to a
given traditional subject? It is no easy matter to
appraise Milton's debt to the world's literature.

The problem is complicated by the intricate
manner in which several influences blend. Instances have already been noted in which the *Bible*
and Homer or Virgil contribute together to the
thought of the English epic. In the same way,
influences from the classics and the Renaissance
mingle, and Spenser's poems can hardly be considered in this connection apart from Tasso's and
Ariosto's. One very significant instance of such
dual influence is given in Milton's own words in
the *Apology for Smectymnuus:* "Thus from the
laureate fraternity of poets, riper years and the
ceaseless round of study and reading led me to

the shady spaces of philosophy; but chiefly to the divine volumes of Plato, and his equal Xenophon: when, if I should tell ye what I learnt of chastity and love, I mean that which is truly so, whose charming cup is only virtue . . . it might be worth your listening." Here Milton attributes to the influence of these Greek teachers traits of character that we might ascribe solely to the *Bible* and his Christian environment; humanism and Puritanism cooperate in his development. Seldom in Milton's work can a single influence be studied apart from the rest.

Consequently, the problem of determining Milton's exact relation to the influences that formed his mind and character is largely psychological. *Samson Agonistes*, for example, is the product of Milton's understanding of Biblical story; of his creative insight into Greek tragedy; of his Hebraic trend of thought; and of the sad experiences through which he had passed. But *Samson Agonistes* can not be analyzed quantitatively to determine the exact proportion of each influence in its composition. The play is the expression of the whole man — his mind, his character, and his deeds, and the best understanding of it comes from a sympathetic knowledge of its author. So it is with *Paradise Lost*. The influences that contributed to its growth were many; but all were thoroughly a part of Milton's personality, and the epic expresses the whole mental and emotional life of its author.

To conceive of a *Paradise Lost*, therefore, or
indeed of any portion of Milton's work, destitute
of all evidence of his wide knowledge, would be
impossible. How nonsensical, then, is Macaulay's
theory that Milton's learning was a handicap to
him. To be sure, learning never made a true poet.
But it did not take from Milton his innate sense
of the world's beauty, his sympathy for the nobler
aspirations of the heart, or the ear, delicately
attuned to all the varied harmonies that words
can produce. His poems are allusive in the extreme and demand wide knowledge of the reader.
Paradise Lost, especially, is a vast storehouse of
learning; but even more it is a work of art.

Such a study of Milton's learning brings to
mind the interesting argument that fills much of
the last book of *Paradise Regained*. As a final
temptation, after other attempts to mislead Christ
have failed, Satan urges him to sacrifice all else
for wisdom, through which universal dominion
over men can be gained. Satan warns Christ
that all knowledge is not summed up in the *Bible*,
and that if one wishes either to profit from the
wisdom of the ancients or to guard against their
errors, one must read widely in their works. The
tempter mentions Homer, the Grecian orators and
philosophers, and the writers of Attic tragedy,
those

> Teachers best
> Of moral prudence, with delight received
> In brief sententious precepts, while they treat
> Of fate, and chance, and change in human life.

None of these sources of knowledge and guidance had been neglected by Milton. But although he saw truth in Satan's arguments, the reply he attributes to Christ shows his disapproval of the tempter's conclusions. There may be much good in pagan literature, Christ admits; for some "light of nature" shone among the Gentiles even after the fall. But there is also much that is false in even their greatest work; the pagan philosophers saw truth but partially, and the poets recommended the wrong ideals of life. Hebrew literature, on the contrary, is altogether of God's inspiration and contains unalloyed truth. Hebrew poets surpass the pagan poets, and the prophets give sounder advice than the Attic orators on the right governing of nations; in the prophetic books

> Is plainest taught, and easiest learnt,
> What makes a nation happy, and keeps it so,
> What ruins kingdoms, and lays cities flat.

These are Milton's own opinions, to be sure, at a moment when Puritanism held complete ascendancy over humanism. But it is the general attitude of the speaker toward learning that is of especial pertinence. In reply to Satan, Christ asserts:

> However, many books,
> Wise men have said, are wearisome; who reads
> Incessantly, and to his reading brings not
> A spirit and judgment equal or superior,
> (And what he brings what needs he elsewhere seek?)
> Uncertain and unsettled still remains,
> Deep-versed in books and shallow in himself,

> Crude or intoxicate, collecting toys
> And trifles for choice matters, worth a sponge,
> As children gathering pebbles on the shore.

Does not this express Milton's idea of true knowledge? A complete education he defined as "that which fits a man to perform justly, skilfully, and magnanimously all the offices, both private and public, of peace and war." The truly learned man, therefore, knows how to interpret and apply all that books contain; learning involves acquisition, assimilation, and wise action. This was Milton's ideal of scholarship, and who would say that it is not to be found in *Paradise Lost?*

Chapter VI

The Theme of *Paradise Lost* [1]

READERS of *Paradise Lost* have always been interested by Voltaire's comment in the *Essai sur la Poésie Épique*, that French people are inclined to laugh when they are told that England has an epic in which Satan struggles against God and a serpent persuades a woman to eat an apple. Such matter, Voltaire explains, seems in France suitable only for farce. More careful readers, however, may remember that in *Paradise Lost* only Satan, in the moment immediately preceding his degradation, regards the eating of the forbidden fruit as a subject for mirth. All else abhor the crime; angels flee back to heaven in terror, the guilty pair cower before even their own reproaches, and the very face of nature changes. Clearly, the eating of the apple possesses some deep significance and must be interpreted as a symbol of some important truth. In *Christian Doctrine* Milton persuades himself that God purposely made an insignificant matter the sole test of man's obedience, since an apparently useless prohibition would offer the surest proof of man's

[1] This chapter should not be read without reference to the discussion on pages 99–103, 111–130, 139–140.

obedience. But in *Paradise Lost*, and indeed also in *Christian Doctrine*, the symbolical interpretation is insisted on.

This seemingly trivial sin in Eden was intended to denote wilful disregard of divine law. Milton speaks of Adam and Eve as "manifold in sin," implying in those two words, as he elsewhere explains fully,[1] that their guilt comprehended not simply disobedience, but distrust, ingratitude, presumption, deceit, theft, and other sins. And Adam, the guilty one, represents no one individual, but man in general. Medieval theologians were fond of finding in Biblical story such types of man. The parable of the Good Samaritan, for example, was commonly interpreted as the story of man in pilgrimage through this mortal life, with Christ only to aid him. Milton, then, is but following precedent in regarding Adam as the representative of the whole race. His theme, which thus assumes both in person and incident an universal significance, may be briefly formulated: mankind, gifted with high instincts and immeasurable capacities for good, but able, at will, to turn each separate virtue into a corresponding vice, determines for himself his own destiny. One is reminded of Dante's interpretation of the *Divine Comedy:* "The subject, then, of the whole work, taken according to the letter alone, is simply a consideration of the state of souls after death. . . . But if the work is considered according to its allegorical meaning, the

---

[1] *P. L.*, 10, l. 16; *Ch. Doctr.*, 4, p. 254.

subject is man, liable to the reward or punishment of justice, according as through the freedom of the will he is deserving or undeserving." [1]   Both poems face the same great problem.

With such an end in view Milton could not write merely as Hebrew annalist or Christian theologian. He was free to read the *Bible* as a poet, not a historian, and to interpret it liberally.   In *Paradise Lost* he apparently accepts the story of creation less literally than in *Christian Doctrine*, and he clearly values the rebellion of Lucifer and the sin in Eden less as historical fact than as a symbol of moral truth.[2]   God has seen fit to reveal heavenly things to man in terms that he from his own experience can comprehend.   But such materialism, or anthropomorphism, justified simply as a concrete mode of handling celestial truth, must not blind one to the truths involved.   It was the act of creation, not its duration; the fact that God, or the right, can triumph over Satan, the wrong, and not the military strategy employed; the sin of Adam and its consequences, and not the outward form of that sin, that seemed of vital consequence to Milton.   He could have written *Paradise Lost* just as he did had he been conversant with all the revelations of modern science, for his chief purpose is not to record fact, but to expound the workings of moral law.[3]

---

[1] *Letter to Can Grande*, ed. Latham, p. 195.
[2] See above, pp. 111–115.
[3] So, too, Roger Williams wrote in *The Bloody Tenant;* "The

Such a theme, however, is as little theological as historical. Some dogma may enter into the poem; but the author's main concern is something other than that. It may easily be shown that *Paradise Lost* is neither Calvinistic, as many have charged, nor Unitarian. Milton, on the one hand, denies the doctrine of predestination, and, on the other, holds his own belief regarding the nature of the Trinity. But no dogma is introduced that does not bear directly on the philosophical and ethical problem of man's relations to the opposed forces of good and evil. The doctrine of the freedom of the will explains the possibility of evil's arising in heaven and on earth; predestination is discussed only to prove man's freedom of will and to justify punishment imposed for wrong-doing. Milton's attention is firmly fixed on his central theme — the origin and course of evil.

In the story of Lucifer's revolt and man's fall Milton finds it easier to trace the course of evil in human life than to find a satisfactory explanation for the origin of sin in a universe ruled by an all-wise creator. He represents first the original, self-begotten guilt of Satan, in the loathsome figure of Sin, sprung suddenly, like Minerva, from her parent's head, and of Death, born of incestuous union of Sin with her parent. The derivative guilt of Adam fol-

Battel about any Truth of God in Christ, is fought and managed by that most high and glorious Michael, the Arch-Angel and Son of God, attended with all his Holy Angels, the Messengers and Witnesses of his Truth on the one side: On the other side by that great red Dragon."

lows, who loses his innocence as a result of already existent evil. Just as there are two distinct but mutually related plots, one enacted in heaven, the other in part on earth, so there are these two forms of evil whose workings Milton would explain.

It is easy to account for the sin of Adam. Evil already exists, and man has free choice of right or wrong. God himself explains that this freedom was given the angels and men that they might honor and reverence their creator, as they could not do were their actions ruled by the divine will. This, however, seems only a dogma formulated because the human mind is unable to conceive of good without its counterpart of evil; existence of the one implies the existence of the other. But the dogma applies better to earth than to heaven, and it is more difficult for Milton to account for the revolt of Lucifer — that is, for the origin of sin in a perfect world. Milton does not disregard the problem as Vondel does, who, without excuse or explanation, represents one-third of the angelic host as ruled by ambition, jealousy, and even lust. Milton simply makes no distinction between the psychology of angels and of men; and in heaven, as on earth, honor, obedience, and reverence imply the potential existence of corresponding vices. God explains the situation thus: [1]

> I made him just and right,
> Sufficient to have stood, though free to fall.
> Such I created all the Ethereal Powers
> And Spirits, both them who stood and them who failed.

[1] *P. L.*, 3, ll. 98–101.

Milton, however, distinguishes between the guilt of Satan and of Adam. Since Satan fell self-tempted, and since in his crime no element of good entered, his sin was unpardonable. Adam, on the contrary, sinned in part through the fault of another, and his action sprang from desires in themselves not altogether base. Hence Adam's sin was not beyond forgiveness. The poet's main intent seems to be to accept as fact the existence of evil, and to disclose concretely, after the fashion of poetry, its inevitable consequences.

Milton's conception of the fundamental distinction between good and evil seems to be that good is self-creative and ever-growing, whereas evil is destructive and in the end self-annihilating. God, the all wise and all good and all powerful, creates Christ and then the angels. Christ, filled with the power of God, creates the visible universe and then mankind. All this was good, as *Genesis* tells us, and all sprang from good, or from self. Evil, on the contrary, can produce only evil, and leads eventually to its own destruction. The revolt of Lucifer brings, in close sequence, the creation of the realm of misery and evil passions, as the antithesis of heaven; the humiliation and complete degradation of Satan and his followers, symbolized by their transformation to serpent form; and the temporary loss of paradise for man. So the course of evil is directly opposite to that of good. Satan confesses:

> For only in destroying I find ease
> To my relentless thoughts;

and he himself realizes clearly that the one result of all his effort must be ruin.

If evil in this way always begets evil, it must eventually effect its own destruction. Satan, on beholding the superior nobility of newly created man, is forced to admit his inferiority:

> So much hath Hell debased, and pain
> Enfeebled me, to what I was in Heaven.

The final step in his complete degradation is effectively portrayed, and with obvious symbolism, in the scene where Satan would announce to the expectant rebels in hell his seeming triumph:

> So having said, a while he stood, expecting
> Their universal shout and high applause
> To fill his ear; when, contrary, he hears,
> On all sides, from innumerable tongues
> A dismal universal hiss, the sound
> Of public scorn.   He wondered, but not long
> Had leisure, wondering at himself now more.
> His visage drawn he felt to sharp and spare,
> His arms clung to his ribs, his legs entwining
> Each other, till, supplanted, down he fell,
> A monstrous serpent on his belly prone,
> Reluctant, but in vain; a greater power
> Now ruled him, punished in the shape he sinned,
> According to his doom. . . . .
>   Thus was the applause they meant
> Turned to exploding hiss, triumph to shame
> Cast on themselves from their own mouths.

Such self-destructive elements of sin leave the good in the end triumphant. Throughout *Paradise Lost* this truth is expressed again and again.

The angel-messenger, Zephon, once so inferior to Lucifer in station and power, feeling no longer any awe or fear in his presence, declares scornfully:

> Think not, revolted Spirit, thy shape the same,
> Or undiminished brightness, to be known
> As when thou stood'st in Heaven upright and pure.
> That glory then, when thou no more wast good,
> Departed from thee; and thou resemblest now
> Thy sin and place of doom obscure and foul.

Zephon's rebuke is keenly felt:

> Abashed the Devil stood,
> And felt how awful goodness is, and saw
> Virtue in her shape how lovely — saw, and pined
> His loss; but chiefly to find here observed
> His lustre visibly impaired.[1]

Satan may remain undaunted; but his determination avails nothing against the will of the higher power; for against that will he can not move even a muscle.

> So stretched out huge in length the Arch-Fiend lay,
> Chained on the burning lake; nor ever thence
> Had risen, or heaved his head, but that the will
> And high permission of all-ruling Heaven
> Left him at large to his own dark designs,
> That with reiterated crimes he might
> Heap on himself damnation, while he sought
> Evil to others, and enraged might see
> How all his malice served but to bring forth
> Infinite goodness, grace, and mercy, shewn
> On Man by him seduced, but on himself
> Treble confusion, wrath, and vengeance poured.[2]

The powers of evil, which are thus chained absolutely by the will of God, are themselves made

[1] *P. L.*, 4, ll. 834–840, 846–850.   [2] *P. L.*, 1, ll. 209–220.

productive of good.   Seeing this truth, Adam
exclaims: [1]

> O Goodness infinite, Goodness immense,
> That all this good of evil shall produce,
> And evil turn to good.

This principle has been more concretely formulated by Shakespeare in *King Lear*. In no other
one of his plays do the forces of evil seem to triumph more easily and surely; the plans of Goneril
and Regan and of Edmund meet with immediate
success. But the evil done springs up as virtue
in the hearts of others. Kent loses his brusque-
ness and insolence and displays only an unselfish
loyalty; Albany casts aside his subserviency and
stands for the right; Lear forgets his vanity and
imperiousness and learns to think and feel for
others and to suffer without complaint. And as
the good thus grows in stony soil the evil chokes
itself. Rivalry, jealousy, and hate among the
evil-doers turn victory to defeat and leave the
forces of the right triumphant. *King Lear* in this
way is founded on the principle that Milton pro-
pounds in *Paradise Lost* and elsewhere in his
writings. The elder brother in *Comus* is said to
talk nonsense regarding the self-defensive strength
of righteousness; but the poet believed it. With
equal faith, too, he declared in *Areopagitica*, "Let
her [Truth] and falsehood grapple; whoever knew
Truth put to the worse, in a free and open encounter?" Intense idealist that he was, he could

[1] *P. L.*, 12, ll. 469–473.

not conceive of any long-enduring supremacy of evil, and *Paradise Lost* shows how the right can and must prevail.

Such an analysis of *Paradise Lost* deposes Satan once for all from the position of epic hero, to which he has been sometimes exalted. Those who read the poem simply as a story, and possibly only for what the first two books contain, have naturally felt the tremendous force of Satan's personality; for he really has more individuality and aggressive will than any other character. They know, too, that Milton himself battled for liberty and suffered in consequence, and without warrant they jump to the conclusion that Satan must be the hero of the poem and the spokesman of Milton himself. The romantic poets of the nineteenth century, especially Byron and Shelley, with their absolutely erroneous conception of the meaning of liberty, gave their sanction to such misreading of the poem. Hence the statement is often made that Satan is the hero, and that the first two books are the best of the whole.

But Milton assuredly did not regard Satan as a martyr in the cause of liberty. "None can love freedom heartily but good men," he declared; for he drew a clear distinction between license and that "true liberty . . . which always with right reason dwells." [1] A character, therefore, like Satan could not represent the heroic. Milton represents him first in all the might that evil for

[1] *Tenure*, p. 1; *P. L.*, 2, ll. 83–84.

a time may possess; but even here Satan lacks the
repose, the reserve force, that the heroic, either in
Michelangelo's sculpture or in literature, must
possess. In subsequent scenes Satan's loss of self-
respect, his feeling of inferiority, his final degradation, make him a most unheroic figure. And
indeed, as the embodiment of all evil, he could
have been nothing else to Milton. Milton had read
and accepted the principle of the Italian critics
that the epic hero for modern peoples must be not
simply a mighty warrior, but a Christian knight
as well, whose actions conform to our highest religious ideals. This principle was readily accepted
by the Puritan poet, who "never, at any time,
wrote anything which I did not think agreeable to
truth, to justice, and to piety." [1] Satan, in the
light of this, is neither the strongest nor the most
inspiring personage in *Paradise Lost*.

Instead, the fallen angel symbolizes sin in all its
stages, at first powerful to attract and command,
but soon degrading and loathsome. He moves
through the whole poem, in the *rôle* of epic antagonist, as the antithesis of all good. In the first
plot, he heads the revolt in heaven with such
force and generalship that only Christ, armed with
the full power of deity, can overcome him. Christ,
therefore, is the hero of this story — a hero both
in the field and in the council hall, where he offers
himself as mediator for man. This is the significance of his words:

[1] *Sec. Def.*, I, p. 238.

But I shall rise victorious, and subdue
My vanquisher, spoiled of his vaunted spoil.
Death his death's wound shall then receive, and stoop
Inglorious, of his mortal sting disarmed;
I through the ample air in triumph high
Shall lead Hell captive maugre Hell, and show
The powers of Darkness bound.

To these claims God gives ready assent:

                                        All power
I give thee; reign for ever, and assume
Thy merits; under thee, as Head Supreme,
Thrones, Princedoms, Powers, Dominions, I reduce:
All knees to thee shall bow of them that bide
In Heaven, or Earth, or, under Earth, in Hell.
When thou, attended gloriously from Heaven,
Shalt in the sky appear, and from thee send
The summoning Archangels to proclaim
Thy dread tribunal, forthwith from all winds
The living, and forthwith the cited dead
Of all past ages, to the general doom
Shall hasten; such a peal shall rouse their sleep.
Then, all thy Saints assembled, thou shalt judge
Bad men and Angels; they arraigned shall sink
Beneath thy sentence; Hell, her numbers full,
Thenceforth shall be for ever shut.   Meanwhile
The World shall burn, and from her ashes spring
New Heaven and Earth, wherein the just shall dwell,
And, after all their tribulations long,
See golden days, fruitful of golden deeds,
With Joy and Love triumphing, and fair Truth.

Of the other plot, laid in the Garden, Adam must
be counted the hero. Fallen though he may be,
he has through Christ's intercession the means of
an eventual triumph. He represents the race, and
his victory displays symbolically the great lesson
that the race must learn. Christ is the hero of

one portion of the story, and Adam plus Christ, the hero of the second.

It may at first seem strange to depose Satan as hero in order to exalt the victim of his wiles. The greatness of Adam, however, lies in latent psychological powers. Innate in him are instincts that open dimly a vision of unseen powers ruling his destiny, and he implores his angel-guide for further insight:

> Tell, if ye saw, how came I thus, how here!
> Not of myself; by some great Maker then,
> In goodness and in power pre-eminent.[1]

So he would learn the hidden mysteries that the Heavens declare. He has yet to learn, by bitter experience, how man's earthly environment may displace these aspirations by others, which, being not altogether ignoble, are alluring and dangerous in the extreme. Raphael forewarns him that a desire for knowledge, like any other virtue if carried to excess, becomes a vice, and that man, instead of seeking to fathom all the secrets of the universe, should learn to use rightly what the Creator intends him to know.

> Solicit not thy thoughts with matters hid:
> Leave them to God above; him serve and fear.
> . . . . Heaven is for thee too high
> To know what passes there. Be lowly wise;
> Think only what concerns thee and thy being;
> Dream not of other worlds, what creatures there
> Live, in what state, condition, or degree —
> Contented that thus far hath been revealed
> Not of Earth only, but of highest Heaven.[2]

[1] *P. L.*, 8, ll. 277-279.   [2] *P. L.*, 8, ll. 167-178.

Living in this way his divinely appointed lot, enkindled by the consciousness that man "dwells not in his own," Adam is made part of a vaster life and becomes a hero.

Raphael's instruction profits Adam but little. A dearly bought lesson and Michael's revelation of human destiny must be added before Adam learns to bring both his actions and his will into conformity with divine plans. Eve, with what Milton would call a woman's lack of insight and reason, seeks means of evading God's judgment; suicide or a childless life, she thinks, will defeat God's purposes for the race. But Adam, whose "more attentive mind" recalls the promise that mitigated Christ's stern sentence, accepts the punishment courageously.

> With labour I must earn
> My bread; what harm? Idleness had been worse;
> My labour will sustain me,

he says; [1] for he sees that God's will rightly prevails. With this submission comes a great consolation — that wherever God's will prevails God himself must be. Michael's assurance to him is: [2]

> Yet doubt not but in valley and in plain
> God is, as here, and will be found alike
> Present, and of his presence many a sign
> Still following thee, still compassing thee round
> With goodness and paternal love, his face
> Express, and of his steps the track divine.

[1] *P. L.*, 10, ll. 1054–1057.
[2] *P. L.*, 11, ll. 349–354.

What matters it, then, whether Adam's work be
in Eden or elsewhere? The one great essential is
this: [1]
> Nor love thy life, nor hate; but what thou liv'st
> Live well; how long or short permit to Heaven.

This noble principle, which was Milton's own life's
motto, Adam finally accepts.

> Henceforth I learn that to obey is best,
> And love with fear the only God, to walk
> As in his presence, ever to observe
> His providence, and on him sole depend,
> Merciful over all his works, with good
> Still overcoming evil, and by small
> Accomplishing great things — by things deemed weak
> Subverting worldly-strong, and worldly-wise
> By simply meek; that suffering for Truth's sake
> Is fortitude to highest victory,
> And to the faithful death the gate of life —
> Taught this by his example whom I now
> Acknowledge my Redeemer ever blest.

All this the angel reaffirms.

> This having learned, thou hast attained the sum
> Of wisdom; hope no higher, though all the stars
> Thou knew'st by name, and all the ethereal powers,
> All secrets of the Deep, all Nature's works,
> Or works of God in heaven, air, earth, or sea,
> And all the riches of this world enjoy'dst,
> And all the rule, one empire.   Only add
> Deeds to thy knowledge answerable; add faith;
> Add virtue, patience, temperance; add love,
> By name to come called Charity, the soul
> Of all the rest: then wilt thou not be loth
> To leave this Paradise, but shalt possess
> A Paradise within thee happier far.

Adam can now leave the garden to face his destiny without dismay;

[1] *P. L.*, 11, ll. 553–554.

> The world was all before them, where to choose
> Their place of rest, and Providence their guide.
> They, hand in hand, with wandering steps and slow,
> Through Eden took their solitary way.

With these words the great epic ends. Years of studious meditation and nobly planned effort and suffering had left with the Puritan poet this revelation of the ways of God to men. *Paradise Lost* thus becomes virtually a paradise, though of another sort, regained; and the poem may be called another Divine Comedy. The Italian poem proceeds steadily, without retrogression, from the wood of error to the radiant glory of the rose of heaven, whereas the movement of *Paradise Lost* is twofold, from happy innocence to sin and from the agonies of sin to renewed righteousness and trust. This is the theme of *Job*, also, and of the Prometheus trilogy, it is supposed, and of all the highest art. Such regaining of paradise is the poet's real story.

Just one more matter relating to the theme of *Paradise Lost* remains to be considered. If the epic ends with this assured promise of salvation, of return to a higher Eden, what does *Paradise Regained* add to Milton's work? According to a well-known story, Milton's Quaker friend, Thomas Ellwood, handed back the manuscript of the earlier epic to its author with the remark, "Thou hast said much, here, of *Paradise Lost:* but what hast thou to say of *Paradise* found." [1] The objection

[1] Thomas Ellwood. "Relations with John Milton," *English Garner, Critical Essays and Literary Fragments*, pp. 135–148.

is not well taken; from the fifth line of *Paradise Lost* to the end, the regaining of paradise is ever the end in view.

Paradise Regained, therefore, is no necessary sequel of *Paradise Lost;* it simply relates, in different form, the other's fundamental thought. The same thought underlies the third great poem of Milton's maturity, *Samson Agonistes.* The hero of *Paradise Lost* is Adam, who through Christ learns his relation to God and wins salvation. The hero of *Paradise Regained* is Christ in the form of man, a greater Adam, who sets the world an example of victorious resistance of temptation. The text of the second epic is that truth already quoted from the first, which begins,

Henceforth I learn that to obey is best.

By bitter experience Samson learns the same lesson. *Paradise Lost* approaches this theme through long epic development; *Paradise Regained*, whose scope is so much more limited, is centered about it; *Samson Agonistes*, whose hero is merely an individual and not a type, deals with it still less broadly. But all three poems express, each in its own way, the central conviction of Milton's life and thought.

With such reference to its inner meaning *Paradise Lost* must be interpreted if it is ever again to hold the place in men's minds that it once had. To claim an appreciation for the poetry of the epic, and at the same time to disparage its content, betokens an altogether erroneous idea of what poetry and literature really are. The thought of *Paradise Lost*, if it be a masterpiece of literature, must be worthy of its form; indeed, must be superior to its form. But that thought can never again be accepted as a literally veracious account of the creation and the fall; it is doubtful if Milton, the poet, accepted it as such. The reader must learn to see beneath the surface the great truths that the story expresses. *Paradise Lost* will then be not an antiquated version of man's earliest history, but a poetic exposition of eternal moral law.

Chapter VII

Milton's Art

CONSTANT reading of *Paradise Lost* and *Paradise Regained* leaves one with an ever increasing sense of their artistic grandeur. In harmony of verse, in vividness of phrasing, and in general structure, they represent the best of English art. Milton had early learned to look on poetry as Hans Sachs does in *Die Meistersinger*. Wagner's cobbler-poet cautions the gifted young enthusiast, Walther von Stolzing, that, although youth may sing as the birds do, inspired by the fresh winds and the green forests, age, to achieve all that art is capable of, must submit to long and rigid schooling. Native genius, in other words, must learn, without sacrifice of power, submission to the highest enduring principles of art. Nowhere else can a better exemplification of the theory be found than in the faithful, consistent devotion of Milton to his calling as a poet.

Even the earliest of Milton's poems, if his purely boyish compositions be disregarded, betray the care of an artist. Although they possess a grace and charm that the severer work of his maturity lacks, they rise, nevertheless, above the untutored spontaneity that graced young Walther's song. Milton's painstaking exercises in Latin verse composition, if nothing else, would have checked the unrestrained impulse of youth for song, and taught the need of artistry. His study of the classics, too, cultivated a high sense of literary form. Hence, to the English poems of his early manhood he gave an artist's care, as the erasures and interlineations of the Cambridge manuscript amply prove. These poems show a perfection in diction, rhythm, and structure that comes only from a conscious, conscientious exercise of art. Still more truly can this be said of the later epic verse and *Samson Agonistes*, in which one notes the cumulative power of his sonorous periods, the majestic expression of his thought, and the deep, though repressed, feeling. In all his poetry, natural inspiration and studied care work in unison.

Yet Milton's poems bear none of the marks of pedantry; indeed, they are most exquisite where they show most care. He possessed the sure taste of the poet-scholar, and his verse is seldom unsuited to its occasion. One would scarcely believe that Gabriel Harvey and the Areopagites only a few years earlier had made their studied effort to depoetize English expression by bringing it under the domination of classical rules. All that Milton knew of classical mythology and history, of European geography, and of science and literature, are called into requisition to amplify and color his thought. He had the knowledge that the pedant craves, but the assimilative power of the true scholar, also, that transmutes learning into culture, and the creative energy that finds for old truths new forms and new meaning.

Possibly the secret of the unfailing surety and nobility of Milton's poetry rests primarily in the fact that intellect and principle rule all that he wrote. Like the figure of Dante in the background of Rossetti's *Beata Beatrice*, Milton stands always in the presence of the reader. The ardent classicism and religious awe of the Nativity Ode, the love of refined pleasure expressed in *L'Allegro* and *Il Penseroso*, the high purpose and strong indignation of *Lycidas*, reveal clearly the poet in his youth. The sonnets, likewise, express his deepest thought and feeling, as they are roused in him by personal relations with friends or by public events. The later poems, although they are epic and dramatic, are equally subjective; for not even critical theory on the effacement of the author in epic and drama could force him to forget self. With a serene composure that should not hide the depth of feeling, he refers in *Paradise Lost* to his blindness. In the same spirit he alludes to the dangers and discouragements that confronted him after the Restoration. So Dante in the *Divine Comedy* speaks of the ardor of his studies, the bitterness of exile, and the intensity of his love.[1] Such direct references to self are less fre-

[1] *Purg.*, 31, *Par.*, 17.

quent in *Paradise Lost* than in the *Divine Comedy*, and are less important than the half-veiled personal feelings of *Paradise Regained* and *Samson Agonistes*. The latter, especially, is colored throughout by the spirit of the Puritan poet, frustrated and perplexed by danger and distress, but no whit daunted. Nor is it unnatural that Milton's later writings should be more subjective than his early verse; so great a character, thrown back by force of circumstances within itself, inevitably seeks such revelation. This ever-felt presence of Milton in his poetry gives it unfailing dignity and power.

Because his art is never dissociated from self, it follows that there is less characteristic of Milton, and Milton alone, in his early than in his late poetry. What is most truly Miltonic could come only after the full maturing of his character. The exquisite phrasing of *L'Allegro* and *Il Penseroso* and their delicate pictures of nature, are near kin to the choicest Elizabethan expression. We find, for example, the feeling of the Tudor poet in the lines:

> Like one that had been led astray
> Through the heaven's wide pathless way.

More exclusively characteristic of Milton are the words from *Paradise Lost*, "Seems another morn risen on mid-noon." The simplicity and severity of these words are truly Miltonic; it is the "grand style" that is his distinctive possession.

In like manner the term Miltonic, applied to

versification, has primary reference to the epic poems and *Samson Agonistes*. Delicate and haunting as is the music of the Minor Poems, it seems hardly of Milton's own coinage; it is simply the old Elizabethan lyric verse stamped by the personality of another craftsman. Nor would the blank verse of *Comus* be called Miltonic. The masque contains clear and fluent narrative verse, from which the transition is easy to the lyric movement of the closing songs. Portions of the masque remind one of the blank verse of Fletcher. But instead of such fluency, the reader counts as the true marks of Milton's style the involved periods and stately harmonies of *Paradise Lost*. Here phrases seldom isolate themselves for their own distinct beauty, as they do in the Minor Poems, from the carefully massed sentences in which they stand; and sentences can rarely be removed from their context without loss. The looser form of Milton's prose makes all the more noticeable the fine structure of sentences and paragraphs in the epic. Sustained harmony and cumulative power mark the poet's grander style.

Because they never were intended by their author to be taken separately, many individual lines of Milton's epics offer the most interesting material for the student of metrics. Of especial interest is the line, "Because thou hast hearkened to the voice of thy wife," which, in reproducing with only one slight change the words of the *Bible*, becomes metrically most unorthodox. An abso-

lutely exact quotation from *Genesis* is found in the
line, "In the sweat of thy brow shalt thou eat
bread"; and the whole passage, so interesting in
its metrical peculiarities, follows closely the words
of the original. Yet the divergence from the normal line is not harsh or displeasing; for the familiar sound of the words and the purpose and
mood of the speaker, conceal in part the bold
liberties taken by the poet. It is only when the
lines are examined by themselves that their
metrical peculiarities attract attention.

In general, this principle should be recognized,
that Milton's versification can never be fairly
judged apart from the thought. "Rocks, caves,
lakes, fens, bogs, dens, and shades of death," is a
line to be explained only in relation to its setting.
Symonds, in this same way, justifies the line,
"'Tis true, I am that Spirit unfortunate," calling
attention to the "low, slow accent" of the first
two syllables, to the "proud emphasis" of the
fourth, and to the "stately and melancholy music-
roll" at the close.[1] Other similar passages are
quoted by Symonds, and it seems much sounder
to attribute the remarkable variations from the
normal verse to the nature of the context, as he
does, than to the fact, sometimes offered in explanation, that the blind poet was forced to test
his work by ear alone. In *Lycidas* he shows himself susceptible to subtle musical effects lying alto-

[1] J. A. Symonds, "The Blank Verse of Milton," *ort. Rev.*, 22, pp.
767-781.

gether outside the structure of individual lines; the same power is observed in the blank verse.

To appreciate in this æsthetic way the variations in Milton's pentameter lines, does not do away with the need for a close study of the poet's technique. Such an examination of Milton's work shows that the chief sources of variation are three. The pauses are placed freely within the lines as the thought and the need of variety dictate; the iambic, or rising rhythm is changed to the trochaic, or falling measure, with extreme skill; and the number of syllables in the line is altered by the substitution of tri-syllabic feet for the iambic, or by the addition of an unaccented syllable at the close of the line or after its chief pause. An almost endless variety is thus attained; yet the music of the verse is thereby greatly enhanced. Professor Saintsbury aptly calls attention first to the wooden regularity of *Gorboduc* and then to the unlicensed freedom of Davenant's blank verse, in order to show by contrast the unlimited richness and freedom of Milton's artistic verse.

This masterful control over rhythmic form is proved again by the varied effects that Milton produced with a single meter in his different works. The blank verse of *Comus* is fluent and direct, resembling the style of the Elizabethan dramatists in their lighter moods. It is the work of a poet who has learned the art of his predecessors, without as yet being called upon to modify it to suit his needs. That call came when he composed

Paradise Lost. Here the Elizabethan blank verse, which had been perfected only for dramatic usage, had to be transformed into a nearer equivalent for the hexameter lines of Homer and Virgil. It had also to accommodate itself to subjects far more vast than anything the old drama had ventured upon. Hence Milton developed the elaborate and richly ornate verse of *Paradise Lost*, the most eloquent and harmonious verse in the language. In the interim between the composition of the two epics, the poet's character could hardly have changed materially, and we must suppose either that his spirits were flagging as he wrote the later poem, or else that the more restricted nature of its subject made a less ornate expression advisable. Last, in *Samson Agonistes* appears another type of blank verse. In its severity and stateliness it differs from the earlier dramatic verse of *Comus*, just as it differs from the more richly modulated verse of the epic. These variations of the pentameter line, as the mood or need of the author changed, prove his thorough mastery over his medium of expression.

In the intricate and closely woven periods especially of *Paradise Lost*, Milton draws the most elaborate pictures. They are not vivid, clear-cut sketches, such as Dante draws with a few expressive words; for where Milton depicts something in a few words he uses suggestion rather than definite detail. Even in his long descriptions the effect is chiefly derived from suggestion. Two painters

working independently on some great scene of
Paradise Lost would produce very different results;
for they would find in the poem but little precise
detail that could be placed on the canvas. It is
to the imagination rather than to the sense of fact
that Milton appeals; the art of his description
lies in its suggestiveness.

The most vivid pictures in *Paradise Lost* are
therefore of the supernatural. For its power to
stimulate the imagination, the description of Satan
is probably the most widely known passage in the
epic, yet the method of the poet is too little considered. The reader gains first a very general impression of Satan's mood and appearance in the
lines:

> Round he throws his baleful eyes,
> That witnessed huge affliction and dismay,
> Mixed with obdurate pride and steadfast hate.

This sketch is supplemented a moment later by
another picture, which by suggestive phrasing and
epic figure conveys to the eye a clear but not too
matter-of-fact idea of the fallen angel's form.
Further details are then added to this impression,
as the mighty fiend moves toward the solid ground
bordering the burning lake of hell. And finally, in
a fourth passage, all these impressions of physical
size and spiritual force are redrawn in the completed picture that begins:

> He, above the rest
> In shape and gesture proudly eminent,
> Stood like a tower.

By so using four scenes, instead of one, to describe the appearance and mood of the fallen angel, Milton avoids the tedious incoherence of literary portraiture, and, by vivifying a few plain descriptive details through the addition of poetic suggestions that appeal to the imagination, he introduces effectively a character too great for words to picture. Such treatment is a fine example of art adapting itself to its means.

As a setting for these portraits of Satan, Milton describes the fiery pit where the rebel angels lay. Two other portions of what Milton calls the "invisible universe" are involved in the poem, and these, also, are effectively described. Milton's idea of Chaos is based on Hesiod's; but a comparison of Hesiod's simple brevity with the elaborate portrayal of Milton will make plain the latter's typical mode of appeal. In *Paradise Lost* the reader sees the momentary recoil of Satan on the brink of that "dark, illimitable ocean"; then the plunge into the surging, tumultuous elements; the buffeting that the adventurer undergoes as he is swept aloft or dropped to immeasurable depths by the changing forces that drive him on; and, finally, his uncertain progress afoot over the half solidified land to the kingdom of Chaos. A literal reading of the passage leaves few definite details in the mind; but an imaginative reading calls up a clear impression of a limitless, formless space through which the elements roll and surge in a light that is not light and a murky atmosphere that the world has never known.

The description of Christ as he rides forth to war in heaven produces the same general effect. But here, instead of trusting to his own invention, Milton uses the vision of Ezekiel as the basis of his conception.[1] The result is a picture full of color, sound, and movement, which grows with constantly increasing power to its climax and leaves in the imagination the mystery of the unseen world.

Against these imaginative pictures of *Paradise Lost* two others of a quite different sort can be effectively placed. Vondel describes the arming of Satan for battle clearly and vigorously; but Satan is simply a Dutch burgher of the seventeenth century buckling on his armor, for the poet's precision holds the description down to the known facts of earth. In marked contrast with this realism stand the majestic, imaginative pictures of Milton. The art of Rubens, also, though in another way, differs from Milton's. The great painting of the Fall of the Rebel Angels is definite rather than suggestive. God is literally anthropomorphized; the angels become demons, destitute except in physical strength of the heroic qualities possessed by the spirits of the epic; and the unity of the composition forbids the sense of vastness that the poet can convey. Art can handle such themes only symbolically. The medieval sculptors who attempted to represent on the portal of the cathedral of Amiens the vision of Ezekiel,

[1] See above, pp. 121–122, 137.

depoetized it completely, where Dante and Milton have been able to handle it with real power. The same impression of insufficiency is left by Rubens' canvas, as it is compared with the more stimulating scenes of *Paradise Lost*.

In other portions of *Paradise Lost* the English countryside is beautifully suggested. Recollections of *L'Allegro* and the *First Elegy* are brought to mind by the lines already quoted:

> As one who, long in populous city pent,
> Where houses thick and sewers annoy the air,
> Forth issuing on a summer's morn, to breathe
> Among the pleasant villages and farms
> Adjoined, from each thing met conceives delight —
> The smell of grain, or tedded grass, or kine,
> Or dairy.

In equal degree, the evening scene of the fourth book creates an atmosphere that resembles the peaceful, quiet mood of *Il Penseroso*. In other places, where the poet's object is to give an impression of the super-terrestrial splendor of Eden, these details of scenery are heaped together with a luxuriance that makes the garden other than earthly gardens. Much of this description is accomplished by the use of adjectives that are strictly Virgilian. "Verdant grass," "clustering vine," "swelling gourd," and the like are borrowings from the classics that the romanticist of a later century would avoid. Better than more precise phrases, however, these generic terms serve to give the impression that the poet desired.

It is interesting to compare the descriptions of

Milton's early poems with those of *Paradise Lost,* which were written long after their author's first spontaneous love for nature had been dimmed by life's cares, and some years after his total loss of sight. He never allowed inanimate nature to usurp too prominent a place in his poetry; for his art was devoted to higher things, as he regarded them, than portrayal. In his early poems, though, he shows a sincere love for rural scenery. Remembrances of what he then had seen remain with him after his affliction. And the epics show, also, that all that he had read, while eyesight yet remained, of remote lands and distant peoples, still lived clearly in his memory. References to mariners sailing on distant northern seas, or to vultures in flight from Imaus to the springs of the Ganges, show how clearly Milton had visualized his early reading in history and geography. The accuracy of some of his statements, judged even relatively to the knowledge of his time, has been questioned; but these passages indicate clearly how his mind, working from personal observation or knowledge acquired in books, amplified concretely each idea that it received.

Another trait of Milton's mind, as revealed in his art, is its preoccupation with the beautiful. There are a few repulsive scenes in his poetry, such as the description of Sin and Death, the enumeration of the loathsome diseases that follow overindulgence, and the picture of Adam and Eve in the grip of carnal passion. But each of these

scenes has its place in the poem. How else could
Sin be depicted, for, unlike Satan, it never was
anything but foul, and must be so represented.
For the same reason, after the sin of Adam and
Eve, the old idyllic love in the Garden of Eden
must be succeeded by lust. Great artists never
shun the repulsive when their themes demand its
presence. There are repulsive incidents in the
Inferno and the *Faerie Queene;* but no one is ever
tempted to apologize for Dante or Spenser, as one
sometimes seeks to excuse Dean Swift, since there
is an obvious fitness in their writing as they do.
It is equally true that Milton introduces repulsive
scenes only where they serve the moral purpose
of his work, and that he resorts to them less frequently than other great poets have done.

A comparison of *Paradise Lost* with other epics
and with its author's own early poems, may sometimes prompt the feeling that it is in parts too
ornate. The unsurpassed charm of *L'Allegro* and
the beautiful, though elusive, music of *Lycidas*
may seem superior as art to the more majestic
movement and the statelier harmony of the epic.
In *Paradise Lost* narrative often yields place to
description. Hence Milton's poem lacks the rapidity and brevity and simple vigor of Homer and the
Hebrew poets. He wrote much later than they,
when art was already regarded by many as merely
an ornament of the matter it presents. This is
not Milton's view. He rises most noticeably to
the "grand style" in *Paradise Lost*, which of all

his poems is the most sublime and elevated in content, because the highest degree of poetic elaboration seemed to him fitting in a poem, like that, possessed of varied incident, a supernatural setting, and a universal theme. He was not conscious, be assured, of ornament superimposed on his thought, for this was not his sense of true art.

From another standpoint Milton's epic has been censured for its want of what critics used to call "invention"; according to this judgment, the poem follows too slavishly the material handed down by Biblical history and tradition. In the interesting prefatory remarks to *Davideis*, Cowley had criticized all English scriptural poetry for such want of originality, and, if Milton handled his theme in this way, it was in disregard of the best critical opinion of his day. But *Paradise Lost* was composed after long and earnest deliberation. Its incidents are most effectively arranged and connected by the poet, and each great scene is finely elaborated. If it seems at all destitute of poetic invention, the reason is that *Paradise Lost* itself has created the prevailing conception of the themes it handles. In the largest sense, Milton made his material his own.

The same is true of all Milton's poetry. In lyric, epic, sonnet, or drama, as he understood it, he shows thorough mastery of his art. Wide knowledge, firm structure, and the finest diction are the great features of Milton's art. There are those who fail to enjoy or appreciate the thought of his poetry; but no one denies him the gift of style.

The greater the pity, then, that readers in general do not see the real personality of the poet in his work. Because of his intellectual equipoise, which the romantic poets so conspicuously lacked, and because of the loftiness of his ideals, the man has been judged cold and unsympathetic. Were his early Latin verse better known, the world would not lose sight of his capacity for friendship and love of social intercourse. These traits are not wholly obliterated in his later work. But it is true that the great interests to which he devoted his talents, and the lofty ideals on which he fixed his mind, obscured his sympathy with the lighter sides of life. Too much he seems to have "dwelt apart."

As a result of this absorption in the most essential things in life and character came a growing severity of style. Were a single comparison sought to illustrate the change, a few lines of *Il Penseroso* might be placed beside a single clause of *Paradise Regained*. Morning comes to the thoughtful youth:

> Not tricked and frounced, as she was wont
> With the Attic boy to hunt,
> But kerchieft in a comely cloud,
> While rocking winds are piping loud,
> Or ushered with a shower still,
> When the gust hath blown his fill,
> Ending on the rustling leaves,
> With minute-drops from off the eaves.

In *Paradise Regained*, with equal beauty but with a different spirit,

> Morning fair
> Came forth with pilgrim steps, in amice gray.

In one passage the youthful Elizabethan speaks; in the other the blind Puritan poet.

Too much, however, is made of these visible signs of change if they are taken to indicate any radical alteration in Milton's temperament. From the first his disposition was serious and his ideals high. His earliest portrait reveals him as a boy, grave, earnest, and high-minded. In spirit, the sonnet written on his twenty-third birthday, the sonnet on his blindness, and the allusions to self in the epics, are essentially the same. The same noble seriousness was always his. On the other hand, his youthful sympathy with the lighter interests of life was simply obscured, not stamped out, by the years that passed. True, the organ in the quiet study took the place of the rebecks in the shade; but there was solemn organ music, too, in the Horton poems, and the quiet enjoyment he then took in life was not beneath the sympathy of the blind Puritan poet.

So Milton's style and character developed consistently and harmoniously, marking a steady growth but no radical change. There are phases of his work that puzzle one sorely who would appraise his character and achievements rightly. Puritan and humanist, poet and controversialist, a lover of religion yet an opponent of all established churches, he presents no simple character for the reader to comprehend. Nevertheless, all phases of his truly great work bespeak the same character behind it. His style is pure and sublime because his thoughts are sound and his ideals high. Nowhere in that great work is his mode of expression inadequate to express the thought; nowhere is the thought unworthy of the noble style. He is the arch-idealist of English letters, a worshipper of purity, justice, liberty, and truth.

INDEX